BIBLE Crosswords

Collection #12

Evelyn Boyington

Edited by
Ellen W. Caughey

BARBOUR
PUBLISHING, INC.
Uhrichsville, Ohio

ISBN 1-57748-371-5

Published by Barbour Publishing, Inc., P.O. Box 719, Uhrichsville, Ohio 44683
http://www.barbourbooks.com

ecpa Member of the Evangelical Christian Publishers Association

Printed in the United States of America.

BIBLE Crosswords

Collection #12

PUZZLE 1

ACROSS

1. KJV verb
5. Mouthfuls of chewing gum
9. Linking verb
12. Tribe of Israel (var., N.T. spelling)
13. Son of Rehoboam (1 Chronicles 3:10)
14. Body of water, in Boulogne
15. "Can any understand the ____ of the clouds?" (Job 36:29)
18. Note on the diatonic scale
19. Parched
20. Diminutive ending (pl.)
22. "The Lord is thy ____ upon thy right hand" (Psalm 121:5)
25. Printer's measure
27. Of flying (prefix)
28. "The lot is cast into the ____" (Proverbs 16:33)
29. Misplace
31. Subject of Kilmer poem
33. "That through your mercy they also may ____ mercy" (Romans 11:31)
35. Boat ends
37. "The ____ of God is eternal life" (Romans 6:23)
38. It can be cold and hard
40. When Columbus is feted (abbr.)
41. Stagger
43. "____ with thine adversary quickly" (Matthew 5:25)
45. "They could not drink of the waters of ____" (Exodus 15:23)
46. "It is a ____ thing that the king requireth" (Daniel 2:11)
48. Workout zone (sing.)
49. The act of washing out or flushing
54. Crafty
56. Roof edge
57. ____ Bator (Mongolian capital)
58. Three (comb. form)
59. Lea languishers
60. Part of *la famille*

DOWN

1. Used to be
2. "The child shall play on the hole of the ____" (Isaiah 11:8)
3. Sunday speech (abbr.)
4. "I give unto you power to ____ on scorpions" (Luke 10:19)
5. Dry valley or ravine, except in the rainy season
6. "The one who says he ____ in Him ought himself to walk in the same manner as He walked" (1 John 2:6, NAS)
7. Loud, continuous noise
8. Wise man
9. "I ____ he that liveth" (Revelation 1:18)
10. Adjunct to a resume
11. Historical periods
16. Son of Gad (Genesis 46:16)
17. Aver
21. "Thou shalt not be afraid for the ____ by night" (Psalm 91:5)
22. Trudge
23. In move-in condition
24. "All that were strong and ____ ____ [2 words] war" (2 Kings 24:16)
26. Promontory; headland
30. Fairy-tale beginning
32. This (Sp.)
34. Grandson of Sheshan (1 Chronicles 2:35)
36. Father of Abraham (Luke 3:34)

39. Realize success
42. Number of months baby Moses was hidden before his mother put him in an ark (Exodus 2:2)
44. Elaborate dress
45. "Thou shalt be...as he that lieth upon the top of a ____" (Proverbs 23:34)
47. Matures
50. Not polished
51. ____ de la Cite, in Paris
52. "All that handle the ____, the mariners" (Ezekiel 27:29)
53. Compass dir.
55. Part of a century (abbr.)

PUZZLE 2

ACROSS

1. "I will come in to him and will ____ with him" (Revelation 3:20)
4. "The foxes have ____" (Matthew 8:20)
9. Isaac, to Abraham
12. ____-la-la
13. Pole vault or high jump, for example, in a track meet
14. "____ of every sort shalt thou bring into the ark" (Genesis 6:19)
15. Went in
17. Alter, hopefully for the better
19. "And he shall rule them with a rod of ____" (Revelation 2:27)
20. Celestial sign, to Magi
21. Remnant of a broken pot (KJV var.)
23. "Nor silver, nor brass...nor scrip for your _____" (Matthew 10:9, 10)
26. Fowl creatures
27. Nonsense
28. In ____ (concerning)
29. Consume
30. Certain collectibles
31. Age
32. Title used when not on a first-name basis (abbr.)
33. "You're So ____" (C. Simon hit)
34. Confirm
35. "If any man ____, let him come unto me" (John 7:37)
37. Drops pounds
38. Act as accomplice
39. Actor Orson, for one
40. "Ye are not in darkness, that that day should overtake you as a ____" (1 Thessalonians 5:4)
42. Pasture activity
45. Rowing implement
46. Chief son of Kohath (1 Chronicles 15:5)
48. Born (Fr.)
49. Twisted strand in rope
50. "Make a joyful noise unto the Lord, all ye ____" (Psalm 100:1)
51. Came into possession

DOWN

1. Jeanne d'Arc, e.g.
2. Vase
3. "Rejoicing in hope, ____ in tribulation" (Romans 12:12)
4. "For ____ feared John, knowing that he was a just man" (Mark 6:20)
5. Appliance
6. "He was ____ as a sheep to the slaughter" (Acts 8:32)
7. Half an em
8. Icons, perhaps
9. Far from cracking a smile
10. Possess
11. "And Cain...dwelt in the land of ____ on the east of Eden" (Genesis 4:16)
16. Blunders
18. One betrothed to Joseph
20. In the near future
21. Son of Noah
22. "A merry ____ maketh a cheerful countenance" (Proverbs 15:13)
23. Elbow, for one
24. "Who concerning the truth have ____, saying that the resurrection is past" (2 Timothy 2:18)
25. "For I have laid upon thee the ____ of their iniquity" (Ezekiel 4:5)
27. Raise up
30. "Be ____ for nothing" (Philippians 4:6)

31. After dusk
33. Emotional reaction (colloq.)
34. Son of Jotham, king of Judah (2 Kings 16:1)
36. Hirsute
37. What the Lamb opens, in the Book of Revelation
39. Partner of born
40. Over the ___
41. Masculine nickname
42. Cotton ___
43. New (comb. form)
44. "____ thee behind me, Satan" (Matthew 16:23)
47. Chemical element (abbr.)

PUZZLE 3

ACROSS

1. Collected prose or poetry of a particular time period (abbr.)
4. TV newsman Sevareid
8. Egg ____ soup, Chinese classic
12. Epoch
13. Beginning of refreshing brand name that "spells" summer to kids
14. Land measure
15. Ancient musical instrument, mentioned in Isaiah 5:12
17. "The Lord God will come with a strong hand, and his ____ shall rule" (Isaiah 40:10)
19. Where Sherman marched (abbr.)
20. "There is a ____ here, which hath five barley loaves" (John 6:9)
21. El ___
22. Deface
23. "Children, ____ your parents in the Lord" (Ephesians 6:1)
25. Sports venue
26. Prohibits
27. "Cast the ____ on the right side of
    the ship" (John 21:6)
28. Total
29. ____ Auerbach, famed NBA coach
30. Masculine nickname
31. "Praise him with the ____ and dance" (Psalm 150:4)
33. Continent (abbr.)
35. "Take, ____: this is my body" (1 Corinthians 11:24)
36. Fare poorly
37. Possessed
38. "I will sing a new ____ unto thee, O God" (Psalm 144:9)
40. Popular street name
41. "All things were ____ by him" (John 1:3)
42. "I am too ____ to have an husband" (Ruth 1:12)
43. "The word ____ God" (John 1:1)
44. Chum
45. Atlantic state (abbr.)
46. Broadcast
47. "One jot or one __ shall in no wise pass from the law" (Matthew 5:18)
50. At any time
52. "For ____ Christ pleased not himself" (Romans 15:3)
54. Corn serving
55. "We shall all stand before the judgment ____ of Christ" (Romans 14:10)
56. Feast fashionably
57. Hair to ____ for (salon slogan)

DOWN

1. Tennis call
2. Gershwin
3. Pill, perhaps
4. Got by, barely, with "out"
5. Go bad
6. Vowel duo
7. ____ check
8. Hoover, for one
9. Cola brand name
10. Liver or lung, for example
11. Bosc and Anjou
16. Oz scarecrow Bolger
18. Byway (abbr.)
21. "They lifted up their voice with the trumpets and _____" (2 Chronicles 5:13)
22. Insane
23. United
24. "Rise, take up thy ____, and walk" (John 5:8)

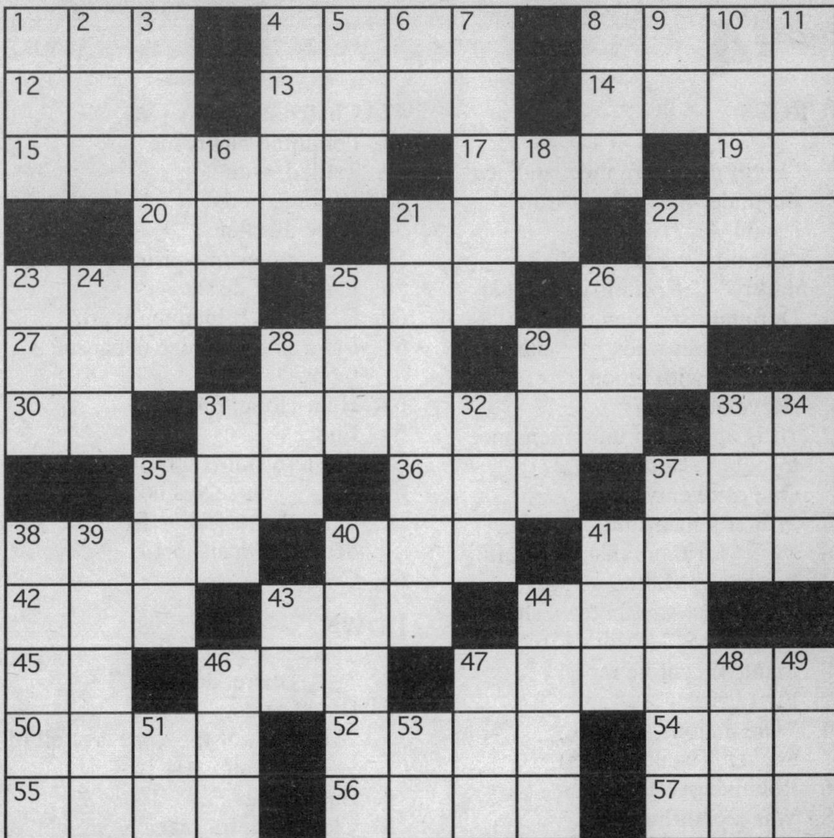

25. Adhesive
26. ____ canto, singing style
28. Make a lap
29. Kin (abbr.)
31. Game where someone is "it"
32. "Over the ____" (goal of hoopsters)
33. "When ye fast, be not...of a ____ countenance" (Matthew 6:16)
34. Fruit drink
35. "The ____ of all things is at hand" (1 Peter 4:7)
37. Brought to a stop
38. "There was a certain beggar named Lazarus...full of ____" (Luke 16:20)
39. Item found in groves
40. Dog-____ (like the pages of a book)
41. Tatami, commonly
43. Midwest state (abbr.)
44. Yearn for
46. "____ thou the Christ?" (Luke 22:67)
47. Perfect score, to some
48. "I will both __ me down in peace, and sleep" (Psalm 4:8)
49. Poetic contraction
51. Apiece (abbr.)
53. Caribbean island group (abbr.)

PUZZLE 4

ACROSS

1. "I will go before thee, and...cut in sunder the ____ of iron" (Isaiah 45:2)
4. "For now we see through a ____, darkly" (1 Corinthians 13:12)
8. Optometrist's degree (abbr.)
10. "There followed ____ and fire mingled with blood" (Revelation 8:7)
12. "It is appointed unto men once to ____" (Hebrews 9:27)
13. One of twenty-six
14. Printer's measure
16. "____ for them that despitefully use you" (Matthew 5:44)
18. "They that sow in tears shall ____ in joy" (Psalm 126:5)
20. Slangy negative reply
22. First garden
24. "The nations are as a ____ of a bucket" (Isaiah 40:15)
26. Relative of 911
28. Was a pathfinder
30. "It is a people that do ____ in their heart" (Psalm 95:10)
31. Cream of the crop
32. Courtroom verb
34. Note in diatonic scale
35. "The ____ of mine apostleship are ye in the Lord" (1 Corinthians 9:2)
37. "Who is this that cometh from Edom, with ____ garments?" (Isaiah 63:1)
39. Simile syntax
41. "Let them learn first to shew ____ at home" (1 Timothy 5:4)
43. "Father, glorify thy ____" (John 12:28)
45. Sault ____ Marie
47. Chafed, as skin
48. Feminine nickname
49. Tattled, with "on"
51. Become bored
54. Cave dweller
56. Presummertime priority
58. Partner of dear
60. Dr. ____ (I. Fleming work)
61. Land-grant college department (abbr.)
62. Hula-Hoop, for one
64. Epochs
66. Western state (abbr.)
67. "____ yourselves unto God, as those that are alive from the dead" (Romans 6:13)
68. Created

DOWN

1. "____ there, done that"
2. Blood factor
3. "The trees of the Lord are full of ____" (Psalm 104:16)
4. Bag or rags
5. Classified, for one
6. Title of address
7. "He that goeth forth and weepeth, bearing precious ____, shall doubtless come again" (Psalm 126:6)
8. Send home
9. Beast of burden
11. Anger
15. Win by a ___
17. Give a holler
19. Linking verb
21. Coin ___
23. "Open thy hand wide unto...thy _____" (Deuteronomy 15:11)
25. Conceit
27. "There is but a ____ between me and death" (1 Samuel 20:3)

29. "A ____ in thy courts is better than a thousand" (Psalm 84:10)
31. "Every ____ of the forest is mine" (Psalm 50:10)
32. Fold
33. Cubs' coves
36. Tune, melody
38. To coat with slime and pitch, as Moses' mother did with his ark (Exodus 2:3)
40. Uninteresting
42. Jacob, to Esau
44. "A Jew of Tarsus... a citizen of no ____ city" (Acts 21:39)
46. Father of Hophni and Phineas
50. "The Philistine said, I ____ the armies of Israel" (1 Samuel 17:10)
52. "A bruised ____ shall he not break" (Isaiah 42:3)
53. "Incline thine __ unto me and hear my speech" (Psalm 17:6)
55. Sped like the wind
57. ____ chi, ancient Asian art of controlled exercise
59. What Abraham saw caught in a thicket (Genesis 22)
61. Exclamation of disappointment
63. Bethany Beach state (abbr.)
65. Continent (abbr.)

PUZZLE 5

ACROSS

1. "But the very ____ of your head are all numbered" (Matthew 10:30)
6. Throws a fit
11. Twilight
12. Changes the subject
14. California time (abbr.)
15. "Carry neither ____, nor scrip, nor shoes" (Luke 10:4)
17. A tree's blood
18. Buckeye bailiwick (abbr.)
19. "Prove me now...if I will not...____ you out a blessing" (Malachi 3:10)
20. Note on the diatonic scale
21. "____ it, even to the foundation thereof" (Psalm 137:7)
24. "Go, sell the ____ and pay thy debt" (2 Kings 4:7)
25. One of Jezebel's gods
27. "The stone shall cry out...and the beam out of the ____ shall answer it" (Habakkuk 2:11)
29. "And I was afraid, and went and hid thy ____ in the earth" (Matthew 25:25)
31. Long, long time
32. Thing, in legalese
33. Positions
36. Getaway destination
39. Adjective or adverb that is the equivalent of an exclamation mark
40. Take advantage of
42. Incite, with "on"
43. Printer's measure
44. A transparent body used to refract light
46. Quadrant in D.C.
47. Conjunction
49. Eagle abode
50. "There was no room for them in the ____" (Luke 2:7)
51. Escargots
53. "David ____ before the Lord with all his might" (2 Samuel 6:14)
55. Touching, as a gesture
56. Member of church hierarchy

DOWN

1. Friend of David (2 Samuel 15:32)
2. "Go to the ____, thou sluggard" (Proverbs 6:6)
3. Linking verb
4. Agent, slangily
5. Kin to comatose state
6. Outcome
7. To declare positively
8. Peachy place (abbr.)
9. Manuscript refiners (abbr.)
10. One who takes to the seas
11. "Be a ____!"
13. "We...are as water ____ on the ground" (2 Samuel 14:14)
16. Like Louis XIV, *par exemple*
22. Libel, slang
23. Pioneer African American periodical
25. "My soul may ____ thee before I die" (Genesis 27:4)
26. Fabled author
28. "Be sober, and hope to the ____ for the grace" (1 Peter 1:13)
30. Linking verb
33. In Sverige, you may meet more than a few
34. "Two ____ shall there be in one board" (Exodus 26:17)
35. Most certain
36. Hang one's hat
37. Messenger

38. Fashion statement
41. Title of respect
44. "Behold a ____ horse: and his name...was Death" (Revelation 6:8)
45. ____ ticket
48. Uncooked
50. Diamonds, slang
52. Oft-used abbr.
54. Bismarck bailiwick (abbr.)

Puzzle 6

ACROSS

1. "____ no man any thing, but to love one another" (Romans 13:8)
4. "His enemy came and sowed tares among the ____" (Matthew 13:25)
9. Greek letter
12. Benign skin tumor
13. "Let your laughter be turned to mourning, and your joy to ____" (James 4:9)
15. United ____
17. "Woe to them that are at ____ in Zion" (Amos 6:1)
18. Actor Buttons
19. "Ye shall no more give the people ____ to make brick" (Exodus 5:7)
22. Lets go
24. Article
25. Explorer Johnson
28. Preposition
29. Warns, ominously
31. Exclamations of disappointment
32. "Another angel came...having a golden _____" (Revelation 8:3)
34. Rouses, sometimes repeatedly
36. Entertaining troops is org.'s forte
37. One or the other
39. Half an em
40. Compass pt.
41. By means of
42. Acclaimed TV miniseries
44. Religion that has a claim in Jerusalem
46. Tribe of Israel
47. *My Name Is* ____ (W. Saroyan novel)
50. "He shall give thee the ____ of thine heart" (Psalm 37:4)
53. Those who trust in the Lord find this (Proverbs 16:20)
56. Continent (abbr.)
57. One that builds hills
58. "Shall I go and call to thee a ____ of the Hebrew women?" (Exodus 2:7)
59. Within (prefix)

DOWN

1. "His ____ received him not" (John 1:11)
2. "Much study is a ____ of the flesh" (Ecclesiastes 12:12)
3. "____ into his gates with thanksgiving" (Psalm 100:4)
4. Reporter's question
5. Brooding bunch
6. ____ *of Eden* (J. Steinbeck novel)
7. Madison, for one (abbr.)
8. Note on the diatonic scale
9. Orange pekoe, for one
10. "With the jaw of an _____...have I slain a thousand men" (Judges 15:16)
11. "He shall be a vessel...meet for the master's ____" (2 Timothy 2:21)
14. "What thing is this? what ____ doctrine is this?" (Mark 1:27)
16. Creative impulses
20. Where Saul abode: in Gibeah under a tree in ____ (1 Samuel 22:6)
21. Solution
22. Zero in on
23. Gets some shut-eye
25. "An angel of the Lord...sat under an ____" (Judges 6:11)
26. "This roll...was in my mouth as honey for _____" (Ezekiel 3:3)
27. Organizations (abbr.)

30. Israeli politician Sharon
33. Not "in a little while"
35. Son of Gad (Genesis 46:16)
38. _____Vic's (former restaurant chain)
43. Rower
44. Mischievous one
45. Army repast
47. Exclamation of discovery
48. Bled, as madras might
49. Likely to
51. Compass pt.
52. ____ Paulo
54. Preposition
55. Greek letter

PUZZLE 7

ACROSS

1. Linking verb
4. Prophets, such as Samuel and Isaiah
9. Occupy; control
12. Suitable; apt
13. Doctrine or belief held as truth
14. Poetic before
15. "____ ____ ____ [3 words]; and blessed be my rock" (Psalm 18:46)
18. Status in a group, slang
19. Decay
20. Loiters or lingers (colloq.)
22. Gets ready to face the day
25. Exclamation of dismay
26. Referred to
28. Greek letter
29. Unit equal to 1/1,000 inch
30. "One load of bread, and one cake of ____ bread" (Exodus 29:23)
31. "If we say that we have no ____, we deceive ourselves" (1 John 1:8)
32. Fifth or Park, e.g.
33. "When thou prayest, ____ into thy closet" (Matthew 6:6)
34. Act stubbornly
35. Orderly
37. Puts aside
38. Option at car dealership
39. City near Bethel
40. "____ ____ ____ [3 words], O my soul. While I live will I praise" (Psalm 146:1, 2)
48. Owns
49. "The house was filled with the ____ of the ointment" (John 12:3)
50. Western Native American
51. Chemical ending
52. Memos
53. Button on the VCR (abbr.)

DOWN

1. "The servant of the Lord must...be...____ to teach" (2 Timothy 2:24)
2. Stadium sound
3. "The ____ God is thy refuge" (Deuteronomy 33:27)
4. Organ options
5. Poetic contraction
6. "Mark the perfect man...for the ____ of that man is peace" (Psalm 37:37)
7. Kin (abbr.)
8. "They ____ up the people, and the elders, and the scribes" (Acts 6:12)
9. Certain sports competitions
10. "Rabbi, thou ____ the Son of God" (John 1:49)
11. O.T. minor prophet (abbr.)
16. "The ____ of the lame are not equal" (Proverbs 26:7)
17. "The earth was without form, and ____" (Genesis 1:2)
20. In the Book of Esther, Mordecai's nemesis
21. "In Christ shall all be made ____" (1 Corinthians 15:22)
22. Son of Hezekiah (Ezra 2:16)
23. John on Patmos, for example
24. Is unable to swim
26. Bigger than a borough
27. Destination *pour les vacances*
30. "There was a dead man carried out, the ____ ____ [2 words] of his mother" (Luke 7:12)

31. "My spirit hath rejoiced in God my ____" (Luke 1:47)
33. Ornamental case
34. Idol of the Phoenicians and Tyrians
36. "Those that walk in pride he is able to ____" (Daniel 4:37)
40. Greek letter
41. Tore
42. Tokyo, formerly
43. Young one
44. Tint
45. Sounds of hesitation
46. Highway (abbr.)
47. "They shall wet thee with the ____ of heaven" (Daniel 4:25)

PUZZLE 8

ACROSS

1. Insect indicated in Deuteronomy 1:44
4. Clothes
8. Book division
12. Son of Abijam and good king of Judah
13. Medicinal plant
14. One of David's valiant men: ____ the Ahohite (1 Chronicles 11:29)
15. Affirmative
16. Blue or White
17. Sets goals
18. "For he is Lord of lords, and ____ ____ ____ [3 words]" (Revelation 17:14)
21. Members of conger family
22. "His bones are like bars of ____" (Job 40:18)
23. Debris
25. African antelope
26. Apiece (abbr.)
28. "The ____ are a people not strong" (Proverbs 30:25)
29. Child's play
30. Fine-feathered filler
32. Empire state (abbr.)
33. Reporter's question
34. Pulled along
35. "The day dawn, and the day ____ arise in your hearts" (2 Peter 1:19)
37. Horse or brake
38. Powerful acclamation of Jesus [3 words] (1 Timothy 6)
41. Add to the payroll
42. Father of Amos (Luke 3:25)
43. Shanty
45. Before (prefix)
46. Priest who "brought the law" (Nehemiah 8)
47. Wrath
48. Postparty scene
49. Quadrant of D.C.
50. "Be strong, and quit yourselves like ____" (1 Samuel 4:9)

DOWN

1. Hudson, for one
2. "He called the name of the well ___; because they strove with him" (Genesis 26:20)
3. Most direct, as a route
4. To make a knot
5. Medleys
6. Volkswagen vehicle
7. "I come ____ fruit on this fig tree, and find none" (Luke 13:7)
8. _____forte
9. Straighten, as a column
10. Drives into
11. Poetic contraction
19. New Jersey pros
20. Son of Caleb (1 Chronicles 4:15)
23. Pale
24. "If ____ of you lack wisdom, let him ask of God" (James 1:5)
25. Enola ___
26. Nathan told David the story of the ____ lamb
27. Conjunction
29. "By him were all things created... whether they be _____, or dominions" (Colossians 1:16)
30. "Behold, the judge standeth before the ____" (James 5:9)
31. "One was brought unto him, which ____ ____ [2 words] ten thousand talents" (Matthew 18:24)
33. Lump sum
34. Doubting disciple

35. Sifts, like socks
36. Ash, and others
37. Disparaging remark
38. "Their ____ is gone out through all the earth" (Psalm 19:4)
39. Bother
40. "Be ye ____ of this, that the kingdom of God is come nigh unto you" (Luke 10:11)
41. Son of Noah
44. "Your father hath deceived me, and changed my wages ____ times" (Genesis 31:7)

PUZZLE 9

ACROSS

1. Deface
4. A seal or official stamp
8. Like a black pearl
12. Poetic before
13. Aesop's foolish fellow
14. Great Lake
15. Masculine nickname
16. Son of Jerahmeel (1 Chronicles 2:25)
17. Darius the ____, one-time ruler of Babylon
18. Far ___
20. Bane of insomniacs (pl.)
22. Grammar-school essay
24. Liquid measure
25. "They may teach the young ____ to be sober" (Titus 2:4)
26. Sheltered side
27. FBI agent, familiarly
30. Symbolic sign
31. Owns
32. Harsh breathing
33. Meditation by preacher (abbr.)
34. "My house shall be called the house of prayer; but ye have made it a ____ of thieves" (Matthew 21:13)
35. "Thou shalt not bear ____ witness" (Exodus 20:16)
36. Trench surrounding fortified place
37. "So I sware in my wrath, They shall not ____ into my rest" (Hebrews 3:11)
38. "Except ye ____, ye shall all likewise perish" (Luke 13:3)
41. Make a judgment
42. "The fire shall ____ be burning upon the altar" (Leviticus 6:13)
43. "Father, save me from this _____" (John 12:27)
45. River or Sea
48. Close by
49. Ultimatum word
50. Blunder
51. "I beseech thee, look upon my son: for he is mine ____ child" (Luke 9:38)
52. "For ye have ____ of patience" (Hebrews 10:36)
53. Actress Laraine

DOWN

1. "They...found the colt tied by the door...where two ways ____" (Mark 11:4)
2. Linking verb
3. "I know that my ____liveth" (Job 19:25)
4. "A good name is rather to be ____ than great riches" (Proverbs 22:1)
5. "Then shall the lame man leap as an ____" (Isaiah 35:6)
6. Mine find
7. Common cents
8. Forgive or pardon
9. Greek god of war
10. Let it ___
11. Shoe sizes
19. "For all the promises of God in him are yea, and in him ____" (2 Corinthians 1:20)
21. "One thousand shall flee at the rebuke of ____" (Isaiah 30:17)
22. Jesus sent His disciples out by ____ (Mark 6:7)
23. Base in baseball
24. "They shall ____ vineyards, but not drink the wine thereof" (Zephaniah 1:13)
27. Wavered

28. In addition
29. *The* ____ *Slayer* (J. F. Cooper novel)
31. "The idols of the ____ are silver and gold" (Psalm 135:15)
32. Throw a fit
34. Puzo's Corleone
35. "The Lord...is to be ____ above all gods" (1 Chronicles 16:25)
36. "A ____ heart maketh a cheerful countenance" (Proverbs 15:13)
38. First woman to be U.S. Attorney General
39. "Let me be weighed in an ____ balance" (Job 31:6)
40. Ring out
41. Masquerade of sorts
44. Corrida cry
46. Age
47. "He turneth...the watersprings into ____ ground" (Psalm 107:33)

PUZZLE 10

ACROSS

1. "Except I shall see in his hands the print of the ____" (John 20:25)
6. "Bring forth...every living thing...that they may ____ abundantly" (Genesis 8:17)
11. "Take heed and beware of the ____ of the Pharisees" (Matthew 16:6)
12. Occupied an apartment
14. More than a kernel
15. Wife of Abram
17. Tavern brew
18. Mideast dialect (abbr.)
19. "____ up a child in the way he should go" (Proverbs 22:6)
20. Buffalo college
21. "The ____ of the temple was rent in twain" (Matthew 27:51)
24. "This gospel...shall be preached in all the world...and then shall the ____ come" (Matthew 24:14)
25. 1,061, to Claudius
27. Bloopers
29. "Ye shall appoint you cities...of refuge...that the ____ may flee thither" (Numbers 35:11)
31. Cereal grain
32. Son of Bela (Numbers 26:40)
33. Grouped together
36. Claudius ____, who wrote a letter to Felix on Paul's behalf (Acts 23:26)
39. ____ is more
40. The Gilded Age, for one
42. Say "whoa"
43. Printer's measure
44. Shasta ___
46. Hawkeye state (abbr.)
47. Red, for one
49. "I am ____ and Omega" (Revelation 22:13)
50. Put it in writing
51. English or western, in the tack room
53. Item to do
55. "The angels shall come forth, and ____ the wicked from among the just" (Matthew 13:49)
56. Tizzies

DOWN

1. "Now is our salvation ____ than when we believed" (Romans 13:11)
2. Rhine tributary
3. Patient adjunct, in hospital (abbr.)
4. For fear that
5. "But they [other nations] shall be ____ and traps unto you" (Joshua 23:13)
6. "French" is one style of these
7. Slow down or stop
8. Fourteenth letter of the alphabet
9. Greek letter
10. Super-duper
11. "For thou wilt not ____ my soul in hell" (Psalm 16:10)
13. King of Eglon (Joshua 10:3)
16. Headed for the hills
22. Golfer's gear
23. Large quantities
25. Mystery writer Ngaio
26. Seller of purple from Thyatira
28. Highway (abbr.)
30. "Now I ____ me down..."
33. "I will ____ thy name for ever and ever" (Psalm 145:1)
34. Man sick with the palsy for eight years (Acts 9)
35. Wheeler follower

36. Speaks angrily, with "out"
37. Not citizens
38. "Put on the whole armour of God, that ye may be able to ____ against the wiles of the devil" (Ephesians 6:11)
41. Tear
44. Roy's partner
45. Storyteller's specialty
48. Summer drink
50. Almost too reasonable, as an excuse
52. Wounded ex-soldier (abbr.)
54. Eastern U.S. state

PUZZLE 11

ACROSS

1. Linking verb
4. Makes like the sun
9. Possesses
12. Insane
13. Lovable nerd on TV's "Family Matters"
14. Honest one
15. French conjunction
16. Land from which the Lord will recover the remnant of His people (Isaiah 11:11)
18. Live for the moment
19. Like food and clothing
21. Held with a certain tool
23. Frost, for one
25. Pitch in
26. High priest in Shiloh
28. More reliable
30. Director Lupino
33. Poetic contraction
34. "Then ____ brought out silver and gold out of the treasures of the house of the Lord" (2 Chronicles 16:2)
35. Spat
36. Likely
37. TV's "Get ___"
39. Frozen water
40. "Thy word is a ____ unto my feet" (Psalm 119:105)
42. "And he...cast him into prison, till he should pay the ____" (Matthew 18:30)
44. At a certain location
46. Organic substance from plants
49. Concerning
50. "While the bridegroom ____ they all slumbered and slept" (Matthew 25:5)
54. Therefore
55. Vein contents
57. What hobos rode
58. In the manner of
59. Benign skin tumor
60. Lacking originality
61. O.T. book (abbr.)

DOWN

1. So be it
2. Per diem, for one
3. Before PCs, one who used a blue pencil (abbr.)
4. Particular potato
5. April correspondent (abbr.)
6. TV's "____ King"
7. Poetic contraction
8. Splinter
9. Half a laugh
10. French cleric
11. "He that goeth forth and weepeth, bearing precious ____" (Psalm 126:6)
16. "Why make ye this ____, and weep?" (Mark 5:39)
17. To pain, discomfort, or trouble
20. Letter from Paul
22. "Who maketh his angels ____; his ministers a flaming fire" (Psalm 104:4)
24. Trudge along
25. "I cannot hold my peace, because thou hast ____, O my soul, the sound of the trumpet" (Jeremiah 4:19)
26. Greek letter
27. ____ service
29. Team _____, e.g., at the Olympics
31. Halliday, for one
32. Reverence
37. Rips one's reputation

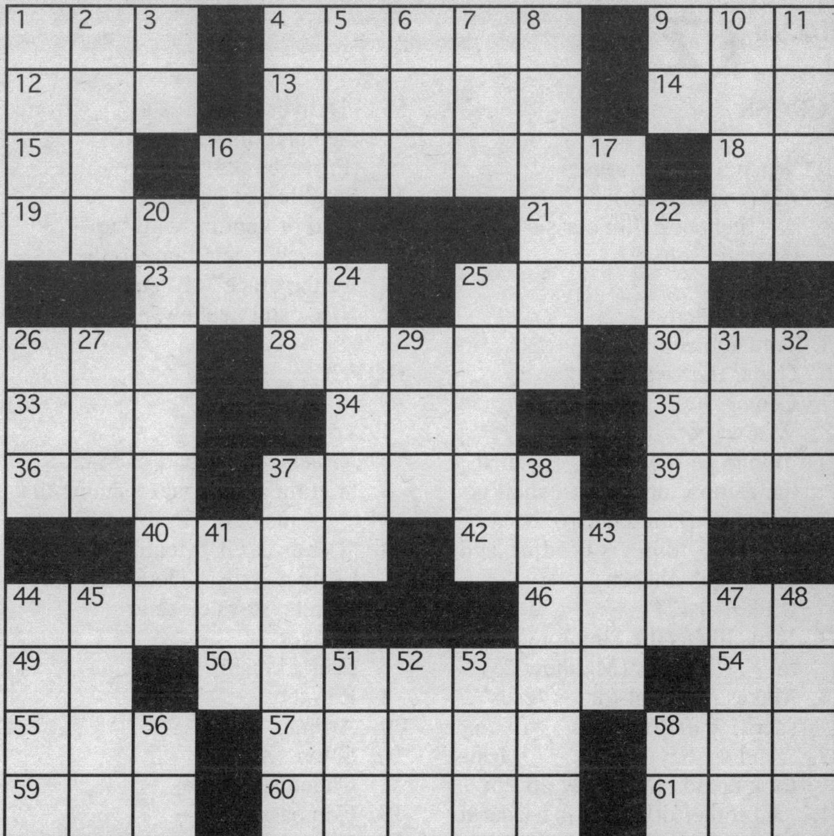

38. Feminine name (var.)
41. Masculine nickname
43. "Arise, take up thy ____, and go unto thine house" (Matthew 9:6)
44. Believe or think (arch.)
45. In or at this place
47. Man, for one
48. Father of Japheth
51. Tell on
52. Inlet
53. Feeling poorly
56. ___-Gedi, city of Judah (Joshua 15)
58. Article

PUZZLE 12

ACROSS

1. When a rooster rouses
5. Air (comb. form)
8. A. Hitchcock film classic
12. Operatic solo
13. Busy one
14. First garden
15. Tree house
16. Under the weather
17. Center
18. Was wary, with "away"
20. "When ye blow an ____, then the camps...on the east shall go forward" (Numbers 10:5)
22. "But ____ thing is needful: and Mary hath chosen" (Luke 10:42)
23. Jesus likens the kingdom of God to ____ virgins (Matthew 25)
24. Makes payment for, as Jesus' sacrifice on the cross
27. "And as they were _____, Jesus took bread" (Matthew 26:26)
31. "A brother offended is harder to be ____ than a strong city" (Proverbs 18:19)
32. ___classical style
33. Let go
37. Saul's exit "vehicle" out of Damascus (Acts 9)
40. Body part of priest on which the ram's blood was sprinkled (Exodus 29:20)
41. Employ
42. Times to "catch the worm"
44. Experienced labored breathing
47. Experience ennui
48. Where the good Samaritan left the wounded man
50. Lions' den
52. Sheltered side, nautically
53. "Deliver thyself as a ____ from the hand of the hunter" (Proverbs 6:5)
54. Firstborn of Isaac
55. Held or kept in, with "up"
56. "Be sober, and hope to the ____ for the grace" (1 Peter 1:13)
57. Niece and nephew, e.g. (abbr.)

DOWN

1. Tribe of Israel
2. Greek counterpart of Mars
3. "Let them be...put to shame that ____ me evil" (Psalm 40:14)
4. "Let us cut it [Moab] off from being a _____" (Jeremiah 48:2)
5. Awaits; stays close to
6. Conger
7. Feel a kinship toward
8. Retract
9. Aroma
10. Salon service
11. Chemical suffix
19. Compass dir.
21. Grassy field
24. A piercing tool
25. "Is any thing ____ hard for the Lord?" (Genesis 18:14)
26. "The sons of...Shamed, who built ____, and Lod" (1 Chronicles 8:12)
28. "He pronounced all these words...and I wrote them with ____ in the book" (Jeremiah 36:18)
29. Born (Fr.)
30. Purchased
34. Mulberry, for one
35. Ages and ages
36. "I ____ to be present with you now" (Galatians 4:20)

37. "The bush____ with fire, and the bush was not consumed" (Exodus 3:2)
38. Good king of Judah
39. Lydia was a ____ of purple
42. Burrowing mammal
43. "____ me first" (former Kodak come-on)
45. "His soul shall dwell at ____" (Psalm 25:13)
46. ____ tone
47. Cartographer's product
49. Forget it, to Philippe
51. Masculine nickname (var.)

PUZZLE 13

ACROSS

1. Director Peckinpah
4. Understands
8. "Thou liftest me up to the wind; thou causest me to ____ upon it" (Job 30:22)
12. Ripen
13. Secular person
14. SW Ohio city
15. "Blessed be the God and ____ of our Lord Jesus Christ" (1 Peter 1:3)
17. "Whosoever shall exalt himself shall be ____" (Matthew 23:12)
19. "I ____ not from thy precepts" (Psalm 119:110)
20. "Let us run with patience the ____ that is set before us" (Hebrews 12:1)
21. "To do" tasks
24. Crone
27. So much, so great
29. New Jersey, to Noelle
31. ____ shirt
32. Dolly's domain (abbr.)
33. "We should be holy and without ____ before him in love" (Ephesians 1:4)
34. Administrator of TLC
35. Fruity drink
37. To be (Fr.)
38. University of Michigan's Schembeckler, familiarly
40. "He [Judah] couched as a lion... who shall ____ him up?" (Genesis 49:9)
42. Where Saul encountered a witch
44. Son of Melchi (Luke 3:27)
46. Blot out
49. "The Lord said, My ____ shall not always strive with man" (Genesis 6:3)
51. Does the hora
52. Act or result (suffix)
53. "____ was a tiller of the ground" (Genesis 4:2)
55. Meadow
56. Masculine nickname
57. Disapproving sound
58. Flightless bird

DOWN

1. "The king said, Is the young man Absalom ___?" (2 Samuel 18:29)
2. "For this ____ is mount Sinai in Arabia" (Galatians 4:25)
3. ____ system
4. Animal not to be eaten (Deuteronomy 14:13)
5. It contains a hammer and a stirrup
6. Note on diatonic scale
7. To mark permanently
8. "Then saith he to Thomas, ____ hither thy finger" (John 20:27)
9. Place inside
10. Stag's mate
11. Bitter or dead
16. Abraham and Sarah were buried in field purchased from sons of ____ (Genesis 25)
18. Tend to a turkey
22. "The heart of Egypt shall ____ in the midst of it" (Isaiah 19:1)
23. "I may tell all my bones: they look and ____ upon me" (Psalm 22:17)

25. Poetic contraction
26. Benign tumors
27. “There fell a great____ from heaven” (Revelation 8:10)
28. Disentangle
30. “Let all the people say, ____” (Psalm 106:48)
33. Father of Hosea (Hosea 1:1)
36. Mother of Timothy (2 Timothy 1:5)
38. “Unto you is ____ this day...a Saviour” (Luke 2:11)
39. Kin to a prophet
41. Son of Zebulun (Genesis 46:14)
43. College officials
45. Restless desire
47. Appear likely
48. “____ despised his birthright” (Genesis 25:34)
49. Game, ____, match
50. Like an IOU, only more specific
51. Show no respect (colloq.)
54. “I have given into thy hand the king of ____, and his people” (Joshua 8:1)

PUZZLE 14

ACROSS

1. Places for the accident prone (abbr.)
4. Things to do
9. "Festus said...much learning doth make thee ____" (Acts 26:24)
12. "The trees of the Lord are full of ____" (Psalm 104:16)
13. First letter of Hebrew alphabet
14. Hullabaloo
15. "The Lord had prepared a great fish to ____ up Jonah" (Jonah 1:17)
17. Consumed
19. Noise or disturbance
20. "Have ____ in yourselves, and have peace one with another" (Mark 9:50)
21. Star of Gigi
23. "The ____ beguiled me, and I did eat" (Genesis 3:13)
26. In a short time (arch.)
27. Swift mammals
28. Conjunction
29. Girl Scouts of America founder
30. ____ girl
31. Actor Vigoda
32. Maxwell Perkins, to F.S. Fitzgerald (abbr.)
33. "For whosoever will ____ his life shall lose it" (Luke 9:24)
34. "I...am persuaded that he is ____ to keep that which I have committed" (2 Timothy 1:12)
35. Edible bugs, according to Leviticus 11:22
37. "The ____ of them which have reaped are entered into the ears of the Lord" (James 5:4)
38. Feminine nickname
39. House or hog
40. Motif
42. Old Testament book
45. "____ ____ [2 words] the Rose of Sharon" (Song of Solomon 2:1)
46. "The good shepherd giveth his life for the ____" (John 10:11)
48. Ascot, for one
49. Less than desirable abode
50. Certain amphibians
51. Stolen (colloq.)

DOWN

1. Type of curve
2. Unrefined
3. "Yea, the ____ hath found an house" (Psalm 84:3)
4. Bird claw
5. Oodles
6. "Woe to the women that ____ pillows to all armholes" (Ezekiel 13:18)
7. Mess duty (abbr.)
8. "Like a lamb dumb before his ____" (Acts 8:32)
9. Dull finish
10. Summer quaff
11. Actor Ameche
16. "The first beast was like a ____" (Revelation 4:7)
18. European mountain range
20. Dried up; withered
21. One of the twelve spies sent by Moses into Canaan (Numbers 13)
22. Positively charged electrode
23. Jesus ____ our souls
24. Duke or earl, for example
25. Isaiah describes these as clapping their hands
27. Shanty; hut
30. "Why ____ thou me good?" (Matthew 19:17)

31. "Like unto the Son of God; ____ a priest continually" (Hebrews 7:3)
33. "There shall come forth a rod out of the ____ of Jesse" (Isaiah 11:1)
34. Mideast resident
36. "How long shall mine ____ be exalted?" (Psalm 13:2)
37. Graduate degree tests (abbr.)
39. Regretted
40. Poetic contraction
41. ____ trick
42. Teachers' organization (abbr.)
43. ____ Grande
44. Jelled
47. "_____, every one that thirsteth" (Isaiah 55:1)

PUZZLE 15

ACROSS

1. "They came to the threshing-floor of ____, which is beyond Jordan" (Genesis 50:10)
5. Highway (abbr.)
8. Bargain events
10. ____ apple (candy flavor)
11. "After the same manner also he took the cup, when he had ____" (1 Corinthians 11:25)
13. Beyond compare
15. Paddle
16. Momentous sign
17. ___-Eglaim, near the Salt Sea (Ezekiel 47)
18. Wight, for one
19. *King* ____ (J. Clavell novell)
20. Went golfing
21. "The Lord is good to ____" (Psalm 145:9)
24. Compass dir.
25. Like some numbers
26. ____ bargain
27. "These shall ye not eat of them that chew the ____" (Leviticus 11:4)
28. Minor prophet
29. Conjunction
30. "For we are saved by ____" (Romans 8:24)
34. "He it is, to whom I shall give a ____, when I have dipped it" (John 13:26)
35. "They shall lay hands on the sick, and they shall ____" (Mark 16:18)
37. Entrapped
40. "So be it"
41. "When he had made a scourge... he ____ them all out of the temple" (John 2:15)
42. David ___-Gurion
43. Action

DOWN

1. Was in agreement
2. Greek letter
3. Mount Blanc is one
4. "He [Nebuchadnezzar] was ____ from his kingly throne" (Daniel 5:20)
5. Stronger than string
6. "Whosoever shall smite thee on thy right cheek, __ to him the other" (Matthew 5:39)
7. Poetic before
9. "Ye were ____ with that holy Spirit of promise" (Ephesians 1:13)
10. "How precious also are thy thoughts...how great is the ____ of them" (Psalm 139:17)
12. ____ Scott, subject of landmark legal case
13. Hence
14. Dry or liquid
18. Judge Lance
19. Taped
21. "I see a rod of an ____ tree" (Jeremiah 1:11)
22. "The ____ shall lie down with the kid" (Isaiah 11:6)
23. ____ Cruces, NM
26. Bridge response
30. "Whilst we are at ____ in the body, we are absent from the Lord" (2 Corinthians 5:6)
31. "God so clothe the grass... which to day is, and to morrow is cast into the ____" (Matthew 6:30)

32. "I will not with ink and ____ write unto thee" (3 John 13)
33. Hesitation sound
36. NYC sight
38. "Let her be as the loving hind and the pleasant ____" (Proverbs 5:19)
39. First female

PUZZLE 16

ACROSS

1. "Will a man ____ God?" (Malachi 3:8)
4. Moon or mast
8. German physicist
11. Son of Seth (Genesis 4:26)
13. Bread spread
14. Dramatic feathery wrap
15. Israel seaport
16. "For thus saith the high and lofty One that inhabiteth ____" (Isaiah 57:15)
18. Time on the religious calendar
19. Note on the diatonic scale
20. Playwright's direction
24. "Is Israel a servant? is he a homeborn ____?" (Jeremiah 2:14)
28. Measure of journey
30. Small space
32. Jellylike substance
33. Son of Abijam; king of Judah
34. "And supper being ____, the devil having now put into the heart of Judas Iscariot" (John 13:2)
36. "Above the ____" (goal of b'ball players)
37. Yes, in Yokohama
38. Saline drop
39. Golfer Ernie
40. Like some egg yolks
43. ____ scheme
45. Many-tome resource (abbr.)
47. Ancient Hebrew dry measure
50. "Minister the same one to another, as good ____" (1 Peter 4:10)
55. Tractor-trailer, to many (colloq.)
56. Person who has to do with (suffix)
57. Protest, with "against"
58. Cut off
59. "He that hath a bountiful ____ shall be blessed" (Proverbs 22:9)
60. Hold ___
61. Three, in Turin

DOWN

1. Camino ___
2. "God hath spoken ___; twice have I heard this" (Psalm 62:11)
3. "Being ____ ____ [2 words], not of corruptible seed" (1 Peter 1:23)
4. Tend to the garden
5. Mountain measure (abbr.)
6. Beloved general of Virginia
7. Creates from nothing
8. Japanese sash
9. Like dog days
10. Feminine name
12. Complete collections
17. Nothing
21. "He casteth forth his ____ like morsels" (Psalm 147:17)
22. Impression
23. Pliny the ____ (Roman writer)
25. "And what ____ hath the temple of God with idols?" (2 Corinthians 6:16)
26. "And, behold, the ____ of the temple was rent in twain" (Matthew 27:51)
27. Shade trees
28. Wizard of Oz actor
29. "Jacob have I loved, but ____ have I hated" (Romans 9:13)
31. "Tender-eyed" woman of the Old Testament
35. Parched
41. Partner of then
42. "The ____ of the wicked shall be shortened" (Proverbs 10:27)

44. Playwright Hart
46. "No man can come to me, except the Father which hath sent me ____ him" (John 6:44)
48. Arab chieftain
49. "The harvest of the earth is ____" (Revelation 14:15)
50. "O taste and ____ that the Lord is good" (Psalm 34:8)
51. Mystery writer Josephine
52. Poetic before
53. Throughout; across (prefix)
54. Wily; conniving

PUZZLE 17

ACROSS

1. Spelunker's domain
5. "Out of his belly shall ____ rivers of living water" (John 7:38)
9. Majorette's must
10. "Ye are all children of ____" (1 Thessalonians 5:5)
12. Tendon
13. "I will come in to him, and will ____ with him" (Revelation 3:20)
14. At present
16. Chemical suffix
17. Off one's rocker
18. "There is none righteous, ____, not one" (Romans 3:10)
19. Biblical exclamation
20. ____ Western Reserve University
21. VCR button
23. "Lo, I am with you alway, even unto the ____ of the world" (Matthew 28:20)
25. Orthopedists' org., and many others (abbr.)
26. "They were swifter than eagles, they were stronger than ____" (2 Samuel 1:23)
27. Latest fad
29. "Yet ____ of you keepeth the law" (John 7:19)
30. Stock in trade
32. Family room, formerly
33. "A time to rend, and a time to ____" (Ecclesiastes 3:7)
36. Mammoth
37. Meat paste
38. Bar Harbor state (abbr.)
39. Preposition
40. "Dear ____:"
41. "____ up the gift of God, which is in thee" (2 Timothy 1:6)
43. Summer, en Paris
45. Coop denizen
46. For ____!
47. Ancestor of Jesus; father of Achim (Matthew 1:14)
49. Tows away
50. Cantered
51. "The coast turneth to Ramah, and to the strong city ____" (Joshua 19:29)

DOWN

1. Sugar, for one
2. Gobbled up
3. "____, and pay unto the Lord your God" (Psalm 76:11)
4. Printer's measure
5. James Galway's forte
6. "My ____ shall utter praise" (Psalm 119:171)
7. King of Bashan (1 Kings 4:19)
8. *Pourquoi*, to Pete
9. Before the West was won, they were plentiful
11. Partner of mortise
12. White ___
13. Capital of ancient Elam, now a city in ruins in Iran
15. A-one
17. "Father, glorify thy ____" (John 12:28)
20. Canary coop
21. "For the wages of ____ is death" (Romans 6:23)
22. Appendages
24. Bore (colloq.)
26. Unattached
28. Linking verb
29. "They straightway left their ____, and followed him" (Matthew 4:20)

30. If the ____ fits....
31. Pursues with a vengeance
32. Mend a sock
34. "The ____ dwelt therein in times past, a people great" (Deuteronomy 2:10)
35. Existed
37. ____ de resistance
40. "Your feet ____ with the preparation of the gospel of peace" (Ephesians 6:15)
41. "Abraham journeyed...and dwelled between Kadesh and ____" (Genesis 20:1)
42. "We spend our years as a ____ that is told" (Psalm 90:9)
44. What the high priest's servant lost in the Garden of Gethsemane, temporarily
46. Have one's ___
48. "Let him eschew evil, and ____ good" (1 Peter 3:11)
49. Kin to alt.

PUZZLE 18

ACROSS

1. Have Midas' touch
5. "God is...a very present ____ in trouble" (Psalm 46:1)
9. Unit with several rooms (abbr.)
12. ____ code
13. State one's case
14. Certain princess' veggie villain
15. "When he had found one ____ of great price, went and sold all" (Matthew 13:46)
17. Debussy's "Le ___"
18. High school subject (abbr.)
19. Kind of gloves
21. Escalator alternative
23. Unlikely hit
27. Take-home pay
28. Between a rock and a hard place
29. Lion ____
31. "Unto whom he said, ____, such a one!" (Ruth 4:1)
33. Employ
34. Title in Tijuana
35. "Yet ____ is born unto trouble" (Job 5:7)
36. Exist
37. Kind of watercraft
38. What it's better to be
39. Fire
40. Defies detention
42. Tide, Crest, and others
45. Sympathetic sound
46. "Give ____ unto the law of our God" (Isaiah 1:10)
47. Detergent name
49. Purple peddler of Philippi
53. Linking verb
54. Den of beasts
56. Many, many moons (pl.)
57. Buttons or Auerbach
58. "Consider the lilies...they toil not, they ____ not" (Luke 12:27)
59. Descartes

DOWN

1. "Stand in the ____ before me for the land" (Ezekiel 22:30)
2. Anger
3. Idyllic setting
4. "I will ____ the earth in the clear day" (Amos 8:9)
5. Initials of electronics giant
6. Small-town America street
7. Actress Grant, and others
8. "Whoso is ____ with a thief hateth his own soul" (Proverbs 29:24)
9. Divide asunder, familiarly
10. On a ___
11. Vittles
16. Sass
20. Prevent
22. Air (comb. form)
23. Broadway souvenir
24. Don't win some
25. Poetic before
26. Songdom's "home"
30. One of the "3 Stooges," and others
31. "Do good to them which ____ you" (Luke 6:27)
32. Addition column
34. "But be shod with ____; and not put on two coats" (Mark 6:9)
35. It usually has a key
37. Prohibit
38. "And, behold, a certain ____ stood up and tempted him" (Luke 10:25)
39. Was concerned about
41. Masculine nickname

42. "In their hands they shall ____ thcc up" (Matthcw 4:6)
43. "It is a ____ thing that the king requireth" (Daniel 2:11)
44. Smite, more familiarly
48. Weeks in a year, Roman style
50. Stag's mate
51. Bed and breakfast, for example
52. Chemical suffix
55. Hospital employee (abbr.)

PUZZLE 19

ACROSS

1. Heavenly being (Fr.)
5. "____ gave names to all cattle" (Genesis 2:20)
9. Get equipped
12. "Who shall ____ us away the stone from the door of the sepulchre?" (Mark 16:3)
13. By the side of (prefix)
14. Talk baby talk
15. Made footprints
16. Arab chieftain
17. Classic auto
18. Looks at a book
20. Bureau
22. On the ____ day Jesus rose from the dead
24. Pronoun for an ocean liner
25. ____ Grande
26. Have a ___
29. Minor prophet
33. "So the wall was finished in the twenty and fifth day of the month ____" (Nehemiah 6:15)
35. Like henna
36. "Take also of the tree of life... and ____ forever" (Genesis 3:22)
37. "I am, and none ____ beside me" (Isaiah 47:8)
38. Ruby, and others
40. Born (Fr.)
41. "I took the little book...and ____ it up" (Revelation 10:10)
43. "For I know the thoughts that I ____ toward you" (Jeremiah 29:11)
45. Rhombus or rectangle, for example
48. Dashes off
50. Poetic contraction
51. Solo for Dame Sutherland
53. "They came to the threshing-floor of ____" (Genesis 50:10)
56. Force to be accepted
57. Sacrifice
58. Singer McIntire
59. "I the Lord search the heart, I ____ the reins" (Jeremiah 17:10)
60. Table d'____
61. High school course (abbr.)

DOWN

1. "Our Father which ____ in heaven" (Matthew 6:9)
2. Conjunction
3. "The light of the ____ gospel of Christ" (2 Corinthians 4:4)
4. "Rebuke not an ____, but entreat him as a father" (1 Timothy 5:1)
5. Mimicked
6. Hoover, and others
7. Exodus hero
8. The ____ sisters of Little Women
9. Seaport in Israel
10. European deer
11. ____ point
19. Classified material
21. "____ the sick, cleanse the lepers" (Matthew 10:8)
22. "I give to eat of the ____ of life" (Revelation 2:7)
23. "I set my king upon my holy ____ of Zion" (Psalm 2:6)
24. Flower part
27. Boundary
28. Popeye's short answer
30. "Thou shalt be a good ____ of Jesus Christ" (1 Timothy 4:6)
31. "The day cometh, that shall burn as an ____" (Malachi 4:1)
32. "____ ye first the kingdom of God" (Matthew 6:33)

34. ____ year
39. Female saint (Fr. abbr.)
42. "I will...____ thee in the way which thou shalt go" (Psalm 32:8)
44. "The law of his God is in his ____" (Psalm 37:31)
45. Kind
46. Understand, in a way
47. Arnie's ____ (golfer's gallery)
48. Make a ___
49. With "of," recently
52. Milne marsupial
54. Daughter of Zachariah (2 Kings 18:2)
55. Hammarskjold, to friends

PUZZLE 20

ACROSS

1. ____ canto (singing style)
4. Queen of ____
9. "The ____ of the Lord is at hand" (Joel 1:15)
12. Mirror
13. Instrument board
14. "The wheat and the ____ were not smitten" (Exodus 9:32)
15. "Blessed is the man that walketh not...nor standeth in the way of _____" (Psalm 1:1)
17. "They that dwell in my house, and my ____, count me for a stranger" (Job 19:15)
19. Prong
20. "____ not sleep, lest thou come to poverty" (Proverbs 20:13)
21. Milk that doesn't require tears
23. "Isaac loved Esau, because he did eat of his ____" (Genesis 25:28)
26. Stubborn sort
27. Holds; restrains
28. One of the Kettles
29. Golfer Ernie
30. Alights
31. "And beneath upon the ____ of it [ephod] thou shalt make pomegranates of blue" (Exodus 28:33)
32. Simile syntax
33. Skin afflictions
34. Wise man
35. Shrinks
37. Fathers, familiarly
38. Burden
39. ___meet (a spouse)
40. Onionlike vegetables
42. "I will ____ the lovingkindnesses of the Lord" (Isaiah 63:7)
45. Reply (abbr.)
46. "____ up a child in the way he should go" (Proverbs 22:6)
48. Before
49. Understand, really
50. Popular Parker Bros. game
51. Saw ___

DOWN

1. ____-relief (sculpture technique)
2. Upon; over (prefix)
3. Old World legumes
4. Exhausted
5. Rabbit's relative
6. Naval rank (abbr.)
7. Exist
8. What Aaron's rod yielded (Numbers 17)
9. Takes away moisture
10. First ___
11. Affirmative
16. Blue or White
18. Hertz competitor
20. Loans money
21. Smudge
22. ____ rate
23. Climbing vegetation
24. Greek letter
25. "Rather rejoice, because your ____ are written in heaven" (Luke 10:20)
27. Reveals, as one's soul
30. "His meat was ____ and wild honey" (Matthew 3:4)
31. More satisfied
33. "The stone ____ into his forehead" (1 Samuel 17:49)
34. "Let your speech be alway with grace, seasoned with ____" (Colossians 4:6)
36. KJV verb

37. “He had agreed with the labourers for a ____ a day” (Matthew 20:2)
39. Bequeathed one
40. Fall behind
41. Compass dir.
42. Scratch or stain, for example
43. It runs in veins
44. Masculine nickname
47. Right-hand page (abbr.)

PUZZLE 21

ACROSS

1. "Sing unto him, sing ____ unto him" (1 Chronicles 16:9)
7. Father of Abraham (Luke 3:34)
12. Hangs one's hat
14. Has a fit
15. Mount. measure
16. "When even was come, he ____ down with the twelve" (Matthew 26:20)
17. Nicklaus's needs
18. "You've got _____" (computer memo)
20. "I have ____ thee with an everlasting love" (Jeremiah 31:3)
22. Atlantic state (abbr.)
23. One who requires taming
25. Cast out
26. "These ____ times have ye reproached me" (Job 19:3)
27. "They call their lands after their own ____" (Psalm 49:11)
29. Gossip (colloq.)
30. San ____, NM
32. "Manasseh...hath made Judah also to sin with his ____" (2 Kings 21:11)
34. "____ tu": how Juan would say, "It's you."
35. Loose
37. French seasoning
38. Before (prefix)
39. Tribe of Israel
43. Energy unit (abbr.)
44. Rector's residence
46. Raconteur's revelation
47. Dromedary, to Bismarck
49. Nicotine's no-good partner
51. Chemical suffix
52. Emulate Daniel Webster
53. Moved, emotionally
55. What Naaman was (2 Kings 5:1)
56. "Owls shall dwell there, and ____ shall dance there" (Isaiah 13:21)

DOWN

1. Hyde Park sight (pl.)
2. Hebrew term, found in Psalms
3. Just waking up
4. Chinese measure of distance
5. AMA members
6. "Shut up the words, and ____ the book" (Daniel 12:4)
7. "When he hath ____ me, I shall come forth as gold" (Job 23:10)
8. "Is any thing too ____ for the Lord?" (Genesis 18:14)
9. Time past
10. Gives; pays
11. Go along with
13. "Laying up in ____ for themselves a good foundation against the time to come" (1 Timothy 6:19)
19. Loans
21. "O ____ me with thy salvation" (Psalm 106:4)
24. ____ *and Remembrance* (H. Wouk novel)
26. Up to the time of
28. "Woe unto you that laught now! for ye shall ____ and weep" (Luke 6:25)
29. KJV verb
30. "I go to ____ a place for you" (John 14:2)
31. Conger
33. Through (prefix)
34. Israeli statesman Levi
36. Aeries
38. More wan
40. Hirsute

41. Church leader
42. Bassoon, and others
44. "With what measure ye ____, it shall be measured to you" (Matthew 7:2)
45. The one who ____ blood shall bear his iniquity (Leviticus 17:14, 16)
48. Cartographer's triumph
50. ____ Novosti, Russian news agency
54. Not left (abbr.)

PUZZLE 22

ACROSS

1. "Behold the ____ of God, which taketh away the sin" (John 1:29)
5. "From the blood of ____ unto the blood of Zacharias" (Luke 11:51)
9. Afternoon repast
12. ____ code
13. Haircare name
14. Lacking polish
15. "Thou hast strengthened the ____ hands" (Job 4:3)
16. "The kingdom of heaven is like unto ____ hid in a field" (Matthew 13:44)
18. Parts of a tennis match
20. "I will ____ mine arrows upon them" (Deuteronomy 32:23)
21. Earthy
23. Greek letter
25. Broadcast
26. "And they came to the threshing-floor of ____" (Genesis 50:10)
28. "He ____ on the ground, and made clay" (John 9:6)
32. Party necessity
33. More pink
35. Avenue, in Avignon
36. Cozy place
38. Turner, for one
39. "The harvest is the ____ of the world" (Matthew 13:39)
40. This means business (abbr.)
42. ETS output (pl.)
44. One of the twelve cities of the tribe of Benjamin (Joshua 18:24)
47. "Let them sing aloud upon their ____" (Psalm 149:5)
48. "The Lord taketh ____ in his people" (Psalm 149:4)
51. Aden, for one
54. Poetic contraction
55. "They...were forbidden of the Holy Ghost to preach the word in ____" (Acts 16:6)
56. Great Lake
57. Arrest
58. "Our end is ____, our days are fulfilled" (Lamentations 4:18)
59. We should love in word, ____, and in truth (1 John 3)

DOWN

1. Before grace there was the ___
2. Linking verb
3. "Make ready quickly three ____ of fine meal" (Genesis 18:6)
4. Soaked up too much sun
5. "Many of them...which used curious ____ brought their books...and burned them" (Acts 19:19)
6. "Crossing the ____" (Tennyson work)
7. Christmas ___
8. "He that is ____ in the kingdom of heaven is greater than he" (Matthew 11:11)
9. Not fictional
10. Succeed the old-fashioned way
11. Speechless
17. De rigeur at resorts (pl.)
19. Thing to be shed
21. "Whosoever slayeth ____, vengeance shall be taken on him" (Genesis 4:15)
22. Texas university
23. Silents star Theda
24. Utopia
27. Chalky substance
29. Steady but unrelenting weight

30. "Thou shalt not approach to his wife: she is thine ____" (Leviticus 18:14)
31. Williams, and others
34. Assess
37. Feminine name
41. Hebrew month (Nehemiah 2:1)
43. "Out of his mouth went a sharp two____ sword" (Revelation 1:16)
44. U.S. ____ (sports event)
45. ____ bargain
46. "Your bones shall flourish like an ____" (Isaiah 66:14)
47. "I will meet them as a ____ that is bereaved" (Hosea 13:8)
49. "Teach the children of Judah the ____ of the bow" (2 Samuel 1:18)
50. Miss. Riv. arsenal
52. "He maketh me to ____ down in green pastures" (Psalm 23:2)
53. G-man

PUZZLE 23

ACROSS

1. Kitchen measure (abbr.)
4. "Let her ___: against the day of my burying hath she kept this" (John 12:7)
9. Baden-Baden is one
12. Titian's medium
14. "I have set before thee an ____ door" (Revelation 3:8)
15. Possesses
16. Evening wrap
18. "The ear trieth words, as the mouth ____ meat" (Job 34:3)
20. Strive for dominance
21. Rows
22. Hardly worth commenting on
26. "Leah said a troop cometh: and she called his name ____" (Genesis 30:11)
27. Actor Auberjonois
28. "They were swifter than eagles, they were stronger than ____" (2 Samuel 1:23)
30. Preposition
32. Univ. subj.
33. Collect collectibles
34. Verses to a Grecian urn
35. French conjunction
36. Diagram
37. Author unknown (abbr.)
38. Exclamation of achievement
39. "Thou ____ up the sum, full of wisdom" (Ezekiel 28:12)
41. Live like a longhorn
43. Leave out
44. Where ship is secured
46. Lake ____ (outdoor playground)
49. Hosp. facilities (pl.)
50. Affirm or attest to
52. Delhi "to go" garb
53. Born (Fr.)
54. African scavenger
55. Author Amy

DOWN

1. Basketball blunders (abbr.)
2. Portraitist's command
3. "He was ____ with twelve yoke of oxen" (1 Kings 19:19)
5. KJV exclamation
6. Elect
7. Spiffy
8. Certain sailors
9. Broken piece of pottery, KJV style
10. Touches lightly
11. Tree type
13. Demetrius, in *The Robe*
17. The family of ____, descendants of Gad (Numbers 26:16)
19. Prince of Wales, and others
22. "I give to eat of the ____ of life" (Revelation 2:7)
23. Torn apart
24. Feminine name
25. Ananias and Sapphira, to name two
29. Bones (comb. form)
30. Big deals
31. Abraham's abode
33. Son of Ahab (1 Kings 22:40)
34. "He that...meddleth with strife... is like ____ ____ [2 words] taketh a dog by the ears" (Proverbs 26:17)
36. Scorch
37. Witness Protection Program gift
38. Was no longer supine
40. Quantity (abbr.)
41. Former senator from Tennessee
42. Green monster
44. Door designation

45. Command to a horse
47. Mouth (pl.)
48. German article
51. TLC provider

PUZZLE 24

ACROSS

1. Kind of walker
4. One that sends hisses
7. What the diseased woman touched on Jesus' garment
10. "____ no man any thing, but to love one another" (Romans 13:8)
11. Capture, in a way
12. Son of Seth
14. Chicken, in Dodge City
16. Accomplished
17. Laughing syllable
19. ___head
20. "They ____ my path, they set forward my calamity" (Job 30:13)
21. Like 911
22. "The ____ enemy that shall be destroyed is death" (1 Corinthians 15:26)
24. Son of ___
25. Oil or water
26. King of Bashan (1 Kings 4:19)
27. "Arise, take up thy ____, and go unto thine house" (Matthew 9:6)
28. "Write in it with a man's ____" (Isaiah 8:1)
29. "I saw seven ____ candlesticks" (Revelation 1:12)
32. "Lord, they have killed thy prophets, and ____ down thine altars" (Romans 11:3)
35. Potato part
36. ____ potato
37. Bible language (abbr.)
38. "Jesus saith unto them, Come and ____" (John 21:12)
40. Funny person
41. "This is the whole ____ of man" (Ecclesiastes 12:13)
43. Masculine nickname
44. Knock
45. Sample
46. Revere(d) state (abbr.)
47. Douglas is one
48. Thing to be controlled
51. Average
53. ___-Gurion
54. Sprightly one
55. "He walketh through ____ places, seeking rest" (Luke 11:24)
56. Breadcrust, for example
57. Throw away

DOWN

1. "They rejoiced with exceeding great ____" (Matthew 2:10)
2. ____ struck
3. Painful cries
4. In a short time (arch.)
5. "A time to rend, and a time to ____" (Ecclesiastes 3:7)
6. Liquid measure (abbr.)
7. Son or daughter, most likely
8. "He that keepeth my works unto the ____, to him will I give power" (Revelation 2:26)
9. "Show Me" state (abbr.)
13. "Their tongue is as an arrow ____ out" (Jeremiah 9:8)
15. Put a match to
16. Tribe of Israel
18. Furniture wood
20. Consumed by, with "for"
21. Paul and Silas prayed and ____ in prison
22. Captain's journal
23. Times past
24. "Whom do ____ say that I am?" (Mark 8:27)

25. "Therefore shall he ____ in harvest, and have nothing" (Proverbs 20:4)
27. "The Lord shall hiss...for the ____ that is in the land of Assyria" (Isaiah 7:18)
28. Seed
30. Part of church calendar
31. Tie-___
32. "A living ____ is better than a dead lion" (Ecclesiastes 9:4)
33. Mother's advice concerning broccoli
34. ____ run
36. Chance (arch.)
38. Item on an AKC document
39. Duke of Edom (Genesis 36:43)
40. Rage against
41. Far from brainy
42. "He shall show you a large ____ room furnished" (Luke 22:12)
44. Tim, for one
45. Post
47. ____ cry
48. Perfect score, sometimes
49. Father of Hophni (1 Samuel 1:3)
50. "Mayberry _____" (former TV show)
52. Publishing person (abbr.)
53. Live

PUZZLE 25

ACROSS

1. Holiday symbol
4. "The ____ of the wicked shall be put out" (Proverbs 13:9)
8. Not as much
12. ____ reliever
13. Object of worship
14. Press
15. "____ far from me vanity and lies" (Proverbs 30:8)
17. Linking verb
19. KJV exclamation
20. Reverence
21. Pantry pest
22. What Nebuchadnezzar was washed with, in the wilderness
23. As thin as a ___
25. Fitting
26. "For my yoke is ____, and my burden is light" (Matthew 11:30)
27. Vase
28. Take in a little at a time, literally
29. Low island
30. State of the Southwest (abbr.)
31. "Thou ____ my wanderings: put thou my tears into thy bottle" (Psalm 56:8)
33. "Look!" to King James
35. Cow sound
36. Gershwin
37. "Man that is born of a woman is of ____ days and full of trouble" (Job 14:1)
38. Pump
40. Understand
41. "Then shall the ____ man leap as an hart" (Isaiah 35:6)
42. SRO show
43. Like a bassett hound's expression
44. ____ hen
45. Of Middle Eastern ancestry (abbr.)
46. "Make thee an ____ of gopher wood" (Genesis 6:14)
47. "Such ____ works are wrought by his hands" (Mark 6:2)
50. Very special
52. "Thou hast been in ____ the garden of God" (Ezekiel 28:13)
54. Kind of lamb in Nathan's symbolic story to David
55. Redact
56. "The Lord is my strength and ____" (Psalm 118:14)
57. Become soft

DOWN

1. "The Son of man is as a man taking a ____ journey" (Mark 13:34)
2. Put on ___
3. "That my joy might ____ in you" (John 15:11)
4. Animate
5. Summer drink
6. Detective's quest (abbr.)
7. Put down roots
8. Fabrication
9. Sound of hesitation
10. Shoe parts
11. Unsoiled; spotless
16. "I am like an ____ of the desert" (Psalm 102:6)
18. Not left (abbr.)
21. "I ____ mine heart to know...and to seek out wisdom" (Ecclesiastes 7:25)
22. "To proclaim...the ____ of vengeance of our God" (Isaiah 61:2)
23. "Ye did ____ well; who did hinder you" (Galatians 5:7)
24. Get equipped
25. Be in distress
26. Take a nibble

28. Baste
29. Jeff Davis's org.
31. Digit
32. Before
33. Haw's partner
34. Be in debt
35. "The ____ fell on Matthias; and he was numbered" (Acts 1:26)
37. God is our ___
38. "The Lord is thy ____ upon thy right hand" (Psalm 121:5)
39. "Paul dwelt two whole years in his own ____ house" (Acts 28:30)
40. "All things are for your ____" (2 Corinthians 4:15)
41. Journey jaunt
43. Dad might be one (abbr.)
44. Annex
46. "____ thou he that should come?" (Luke 7:19)
47. Fathers and uncles, for example
48. "____ of every sort shalt thou bring" (Genesis 6:19)
49. "Though he slay me, ____ will I trust in him" (Job 13:15)
51. "Gibeon...was greater than ____ and all the men...were mighty" (Joshua 10:2)
53. Act

PUZZLE 26

ACROSS

1. "Every one could sling stones at an hair breadth, and not____" (Judges 20:16)
5. "In their hands they shall ____ thee up lest...thou dash thy foot against a stone" (Matthew 4:6)
9. Before
12. Duke or duchess, for example
13. Word in a threat
14. Disagreement
15. Tribe of Israel
17. "So then they that are in the flesh cannot ____ God" (Romans 8:8)
19. This cookie didn't crumble (it's a success)
21. Lets up
22. Outgrowth
25. Linking verb
26. Canola, for one
27. "Joy that was set before him, endured the ____, despising the shame" (Hebrews 12:2)
29. Unit of weight (abbr.)
31. Behold's partner
32. "Behold an Israelite indeed, in whom is no ____" (John 1:47)
33. "They fled before the men of ____" (Joshua 7:4)
34. French conjunction
35. "This he said, not that he ____ for the poor" (John 12:6)
36. Consumed
37. With Aaron, he held up Moses' hands (Exodus 17)
38. "But ____ us from evil" (Matthew 6:13)
41. Maritime occurrence
43. "The third day he shall ____ again" (Matthew 20:19)
44. "Fallen ____ in Christ" (Christians who have already died) (1 Corinthians 15:18)
46. Stop on the journey from Egypt to Jordan (Numbers 33:27)
49. Tribe of Israel
50. "Hallowed be thy ____" (Matthew 6:9)
53. Continent
54. Hospital facility (abbr., pl.)
55. Sheet size
56. Ancient European

DOWN

1. Baby lamb's cry
2. April addressee
3. Take to ____ (or defeat handily, colloq.)
4. Pottery remains (arch.)
5. "How can these things ___?" (John 3:9)
6. It loops the Loop (abbr.)
7. Serpent
8. "Whom will ye that I ____ unto you, Barabbas or Jesus?" (Matthew 27:17)
9. Wipe away
10. "The desert shall...blossom as the ____" (Isaiah 35:1)
11. Part of the pasture populace (pl.)
16. Son of Peleg (Genesis 11:18)
18. Corn servings
20. Happen
22. "Make thee a fiery serpent and set it upon a ____" (Numbers 21:8)
23. Uproar
24. True's partner
28. Longer in the tooth
29. "It is vain for you to rise up early, to sit up ____" (Psalm 127:2)

30. Coffin and platform
32. Item of clothing
35. Find a solution
36. Disinclined
37. What are not barred (colloq.)
39. Illuminated
40. Ishmael's half-brother
41. Wise man
42. Peter, for one
45. "The Lord that delivered me out of the ____ of the lion" (1 Samuel 17:37)
47. To be under the weather
48. Panama, for one
51. Note on the diatonic scale
52. Printer's measure

PUZZLE 27

ACROSS

1. They give a hoot
5. Smite, modern style
9. Time of personal testing
10. "Every kind of beasts...hath been ____ of mankind" (James 3:7)
12. Rio ___
13. Officer of David who "was over the tribute" (2 Samuel 20:24)
15. Cereal grain
16. "He cannot ____ himself" (2 Timothy 2:13)
18. Trigonometric ratio
19. Healing plant
21. Put two and two together
23. Middle-school subj.
24. Egg size
26. One who grinds his teeth
28. "Stand in the ____ before me" (Ezekiel 22:30)
30. Cotton ___
31. God ____ those who honestly seek Him
35. Earl, for one
39. Ancient Scandinavian war horn
40. ____ de France
42. Dandelion, for one
43. To be (Fr.)
45. "I will...that men ____ every where, lifting up holy hands" (1 Timothy 2:8)
47. One beguiled by the serpent
48. Scoundrel (colloq.)
50. "Looking up to ____ he blessed them" (Luke 9:16)
52. Garden or grass, for example
53. Amend
54. What club coffers contain
55. Lunch orders (abbr.)

DOWN

1. "The Lord...doth take away from Jerusalem...the eloquent____" (Isaiah 3:1, 3)
2. "I count all things but loss...that I may ____ Christ" (Philippians 3:8)
3. Actor Alan
4. "Now I lay me down to ___"
5. ____ power
6. Young boy
7. Minor prophet
8. "____ the thought"
9. Singing syllables
11. "Praise him with the timbrel and ____" (Psalm 150:4)
12. Paul's was the high calling of God in Jesus Christ
14. Gutsy Golda
17. What husbands don't want wives to do
20. Served shirred, perhaps
22. "The Lord God had not caused it to ____ upon the earth" (Genesis 2:5)
25. Whence the wise men came
27. ____on-the-mountain
29. "Thou must prophesy again before many ____" (Revelation 10:11)
31. Played certain instruments
32. Old stringed instruments
33. Task to do
34. French preposition
36. "And levy a tribute unto the Lord...both of the persons, and of the ____" (Numbers 31:28)
37. Bar used to pry
38. "All the trees of ____, the choice and best of Lebanon" (Ezekiel 31:16)

41. "They...came into an harlot's house, named ____" (Joshua 2:1)
44. Firstborn of Isaac and Rebekah
46. Make oneself heard
49. Make ends meet, with "out"
51. Memo abbr.

PUZZLE 28

ACROSS

1. Polite word (pl.)
5. Seaport of Israel
9. Nocturnal creature
12. David or Solomon, perhaps
13. London's Abbey is one
14. Nineteenth-century American author
15. Prophetess and daughter of Phanuel
16. They respond to 911 (abbr.)
17. Like food or water
18. "Or if he shall ask an ____, will he offer him a scorpion?" (Luke 11:12)
20. Former P.M. of Israel
22. "____ not at all; neither by heaven" (Matthew 5:34)
24. Period
25. Simile syntax
27. One hundred fifty-one, to Livy
28. Hoover, for one
30. Large group
32. Trite phrase
34. Like one who "hath a devil" (John 10:20)
36. Always
37. "Be ye ____, and sin not" (Ephesians 4:26)
39. Regret
41. Before
42. Movie rating (abbr.)
43. Texas Tech's ____ Raiders
45. Like a foyer
47. Room's partner
49. Just a ___
50. Asaph the ____ (2 Chronicles 29:30)
52. Have a bite
54. After the crucifixion, the soldiers gambled for Jesus' ___
57. Hole-making tool
58. "His clothes shall be rent and his head ____" (Leviticus 13:45)
59. Prophet who follows Joel
60. Still
61. Former British P.M. Anthony
62. It comes with the territory, in the kitchen

DOWN

1. Retreat, perhaps
2. Electrically charged atom
3. "Be ye transformed by the ____ of your mind" (Romans 12:2)
4. ___struck
5. Linking verb
6. Search thoroughly
7. Demolished (as in Psalm 137:7)
8. Sullivan, for one
9. Pull to ___
10. "One ____ is past and behold there come two" (Revelation 9:12)
11. "He was ____ as a sheep to the slaughter" (Acts 8:32)
17. "As vinegar upon ____, so is he that singeth songs to an heavy heart" (Proverbs 25:20)
19. Tribe of Israel
21. "There is but one ____" (1 Corinthians 8:6)
22. "His ____ was in his hand: and he drew near the Philistine" (1 Samuel 17:40)
23. Slam against
25. _____ Fisher Hall, in NYC
26. Withered
27. "O ____ your hands, all ye people" (Psalm 47:1)
29. Deface

31. "But be of good cheer; I have ____ the world" (John 16:33)
33. "He is risen from the dead: so the last ____ shall be worse than the first" (Matthew 27:64)
35. Date ____ (library logo)
38. KJV affirmative
40. Naval officer (abbr.)
44. "Fear and ____ shall fall upon them" (Exodus 15:16)
46. Father of Abram
47. Update of biblical girdle
48. "For I will not ____ to speak of any of those things which Christ hath not wrought" (Romans 15:18)
50. " ____ what?"
51. Lea dowager
53. "Praise the Lord with...an instrument of ____ strings" (Psalm 33:2)
55. Flamboyant wrap
56. NYC time
58. Exist

PUZZLE 29

ACROSS

1. Iowa city
5. Apple variety
9. Thirty Years' ___
12. "I will bring again the captivity of ____" (Jeremiah 49:39)
13. Levitical city of refuge (1 Chronicles 6:73)
14. Samuel's mentor
15. Continent (abbr.)
16. Wired, with "on"
18. "They shall ____ the whirlwind: it hath no stalk" (Hosea 8:7)
19. "My Father giveth you the ____ bread from heaven" (John 6:32)
20. Where the prodigal son dined out
22. Live; realize one's potential
23. "The ____ of wisdom is above rubies" (Job 28:18)
25. "If the good man...had known what hour the ____ would come" (Luke 12:39)
27. Deceased
28. Facade
29. Kind of number
32. Ember residue
33. Trunk "tenant"
34. KJV deer
35. Born (Fr.)
36. Pitchfork hazard
37. Winter plague
38. Adhere
40. Fish or fight
41. Hush!
43. Linking verb
44. "I was an hungred and ye gave me no ____" (Matthew 25:42)
45. ____ and Gown
47. Unplanned information channel (colloq.)
48. Son of Judah (Genesis 38)
50. Used to row the boat
51. Opera solo
53. "At ____" (heard at certain camps)
55. Meddle
56. Be introduced
57. "I am instructed...both to abound and to suffer ____" (Philippians 4:12)

DOWN

1. Number of lepers in Samaria who were healed by Jesus (Luke 17)
2. In the manner of
3. One of the Kettles
4. "And they shall ____ him in an hundred shekels of silver" (Deuteronomy 22:19)
5. "The chariots shall ____ in the streets" (Nahum 2:4)
6. Number of lepers in Samaria who praised God (Luke 17)
7. Bar Harbor state (abbr.)
8. Auntie ____ (L. F. Baum character)
9. Tiny and young
10. Southern state (abbr.)
11. Ready
17. "Let us not be weary...for in ____ season we shall reap" (Galatians 6:9)
18. Deli staple
19. "Bring ye all the ____ into the storehouse" (Malachi 3:10)
20. Lion's portion
21. Horologist's concern, in a way
23. ____ of action
24. Level, as a building (Brit.)

25. "First, I ____ my God through Jesus Christ for you all" (Romans 1:8)
26. Didn't remember
28. ____ Islands
30. Dreary
31. "Let us not love in word...but in _____" (1 John 3:18)
33. Agitate
37. Become aware of
39. Ecru
40. The Great ___
41. Organ option
42. "As small as the ____ frost on the ground" (Exodus 16:14)
44. "I have ____ to eat that ye know not of" (John 4:32)
46. Droll
47. ____ low
48. Compass dir.
49. Buttons
51. Exist
52. In ___
54. One (Scot.)

PUZZLE 30

ACROSS

1. "God clave an hollow place that was in the ____, and there came water thereout" (Judges 15:19)
4. Prepare fruit
8. Whatever ____ you
12. Jurist Fortas
13. Black
14. Dagger
15. "He ____ my strength in the way" (Psalm 102:23)
17. Permanent mark
18. Evidence of beating
19. Sesame, for one
20. Northwest ____ (abbr.)
21. "Shoot out thine ____, and destroy them" (Psalm 144:6)
24. Ate out
27. Linking verb
28. Comprehend
29. Son of Zeus
30. "How can a man be born when he is ___?" (John 3:4)
31. *Dead* ____ (Dick Francis classic)
32. French pronoun
33. Hole-making tool
34. Amusement park amusements
35. Begin a conversation
37. Wager
38. Hurry (arch.)
39. Punish (arch.)
43. Steakhouse selection, perhaps
45. "Though they would have cast anchors out of the ____" (Acts 27:30)
47. Cary Grant, once
48. Father of Azariah (2 Chronicles 15:1)
49. Paris summer
50. Challenge
51. Whirlpool
52. Affirmative vote

DOWN

1. Spielberg film
2. Aid's partner
3. ____ thin
4. "There was none that moved the wing or opened the mouth, or ____" (Isaiah 10:14)
5. Son of Ner (2 Samuel 2:8)
6. "Asahel was as light of foot as a wild ____" (2 Samuel 2:18)
7. Like omega
8. Son of Kohath (1 Chronicles 6:22)
9. "And they wrought onyx stones ____ in ouches of gold" (Exodus 39:6)
10. Bucolic locale
11. Indian weight
16. Unclean birds (Deuteronomy 14:13)
19. Pay dirt
21. Son of Bela (Numbers 26:40)
22. Used to be
23. Cupboard collections, as in dishes
24. Fruit of the palm
25. Smooth
26. One close by
27. Cheer competitor
30. "____ no man any thing, but to love" (Romans 13:8)
31. Refers to
33. Mature
34. "The wrath of the Lord arose against his people, till there was no ____" (2 Chronicles 36:16)
36. Seat location
37. Told all
40. Feminine name

41. Bethlehem: ____ of David
42. Fencing gear
43. Exterminate
44. Lupino
45. Nemesis
46. "The ____ number...is to be redeemed" (Numbers 3:48)

PUZZLE 31

ACROSS

1. This admits attorneys
4. Tribe of Israel
9. Son of King Abijam
12. KJV verb
13. "The last ____ of that man is worse than the first" (Luke 11:26)
14. Atlantic state (abbr.)
15. Exist
16. "Abstain from ____ lusts which war against the soul" (1 Peter 2:11)
18. Apiece (abbr.)
19. Golf goal
21. Golf bag contents
23. "I will not give sleep to mine ____" (Psalm 132:4)
25. Aerie
26. Prophetic O.T. book (abbr.)
28. Entreat
30. What may be let out
33. Linking verb
34. "____ yourselves likewise with the same mind" (1 Peter 4:1)
35. "As it was in the days of ____, so shall it be" (Luke 17:26)
36. Del ____, CA
37. Fades
39. "There was no room for them in the ____" (Luke 2:7)
40. In short order (arch.)
42. ____ man (jazz player)
44. King of the Moabites (Numbers 22:4)
46. Dinner table favorites, especially with children
49. Linking verb
50. Populates
54. Twelve Step gp.
55. Under-____ (beach hazard)
57. Hebrew month
58. ATM number
59. "It will be fair weather: for the ____ is red" (Matthew 16:2)
60. Undergarments
61. What Hophni and Phineas took into battle

DOWN

1. Bunyon's ox
2. ____ code
3. Correct (abbr.)
4. "Where is the promise of his coming? for since the fathers fell ____" (2 Peter 3:4)
5. Sault ____ Marie
6. Possesses
7. Ordinal suffix
8. Depended on
9. Classified info
10. "God hath ____ mine affliction" (Genesis 31:42)
11. Exclamation of dismay
16. Summer pest
17. Time period (abbr., pl.)
20. "To the ____ assembly and church of the firstborn" (Hebrews 12:23)
22. First judge of Israel
24. "In the midst of the elders, stood a Lamb as it had been ____" (Revelation 5:6)
25. "Your ____ are written in heaven" (Luke 10:20)
26. Flood preventer, sometimes
27. Former NFL coach Parseghian
29. "Ye do ____, not knowing the scriptures" (Matthew 22:29)
31. Many moons

32. "Let no man glory in ___. For all things are yours" (1 Corinthians 3:21)
37. "Who sent ____ and wonders into the midst of thee, O Egypt" (Psalm 135:9)
38. Mythological nymphs
41. Part of fabric
43. PC operating system
44. Cavern dwellers
45. Lose control, with "run"
47. Hideaway
48. Went down
51. What was poured on Saul's head
52. Greek letter
53. Sitting down, you get this
56. Western state (abbr.)
58. State College state (abbr.)

PUZZLE 32

ACROSS

1. White, for one
5. "For I have no man...who will naturally ____ for your state" (Philippians 2:20)
9. Kind of truck
12. Minor prophet
13. So be it
14. Female lea dweller
15. 3.1416
16. Sixties-style dress
18. "They compassed me about like ____" (Psalm 118:12)
19. "She shall shave her head and ____ her nails" (Deuteronomy 21:12)
20. Greek letter
22. NY or CA
23. Greek isle
25. "Do ye think that the scripture ____ in vain" (James 4:5)
27. Definitely pink
28. Nick Charles, aka *The ____ Man*
29. Exclamation of discovery
32. ____ *on parle francais*
33. "For if ye love them which love you, what ____ have ye?" (Luke 6:32)
34. ____ fried
35. Barbara ____ Geddes
36. Baby and bath, to name two
37. "And he ____ and touched his tongue" (Mark 7:33)
38. "Is the Lord's hand waxed ___?" (Numbers 11:23)
40. Prophets
41. Athens is here (abbr.)
43. "Joseph...was the son of his ____ age" (Genesis 37:3)
44. ____ there, done that
45. "The workman is worthy of his ____" (Matthew 10:10)
47. Come together; touch
48. "Arise, go up to ____" (Joshua 8:1)
50. Mess up
51. Shut's partner
53. Apparent one
55. Asiatic deer
56. Accustomed
57. "I'm all ___"

DOWN

1. "The trees of the Lord are full of ____" (Psalm 104:16)
2. French friend
3. Biblical exclamation
4. "He hath regarded the low ____ of his handmaiden" (Luke 1:48)
5. Hawaiian product, for short
6. Quantity (abbr.)
7. Concerning
8. ___-gedi (where David dwelt for a time)
9. To a ___
10. Is beholden to
11. Author Nathanael
17. Before
18. Bridle part
19. Pauline's adventures of filmdom
20. "Whom God hath raised up, having loosed the ____ of death" (Acts 2:24)
21. Kind of hole
23. "Where no oxen are, the ____ is clean" (Proverbs 14:4)
24. 3 K or 5 K, for example
25. "Thou ____ love thy neighbor" (Romans 13:9)

26. "He...began to tell them what things should ____ unto him" (Mark 10:32)
28. "The Lord called Samuel again the ____ time" (1 Samuel 3:8)
30. Absalom's stunning feature
31. "The ____ are a people not strong" (Proverbs 30:25)
33. Hand or power
37. Rage inside
39. Salsa choice
40. Jurisdiction of a bishop
41. Ancient Hebrew dry measure
42. Deli order
44. "He hath ____ his bow, and made it ready" (Psalm 7:12)
46. Linking verb
47. "I will...that ____ pray everywhere" (1 Timothy 2:8)
48. Broadcast
49. Government agency (abbr.)
51. Ouch!
52. River in Italy
54. Per person (abbr.)

PUZZLE 33

ACROSS

1. "Until the day dawn, and the day ____ arise" (2 Peter 1:19)
5. "Believe not every spirit, but ____ the spirits" (1 John 4:1)
8. Some circles
12. "Take thine ____, eat, drink, and be merry" (Luke 12:19)
13. Do garden work
14. Wild rest stop
15. Operatic highlight
16. *Mange*, in Marshalltown
17. Land measure
18. "Let them be for signs, and for ____, and for day, and years" (Genesis 1:14)
20. Pine
21. Exclamation of pain
22. Item to do
24. Newsman Phillips
27. Laughing sound
28. Moisture
31. Holds the deed to
32. "We have also a more ____ word of prophecy" (2 Peter 1:19)
33. Forest female
34. "If God ____ for us, who can be against us?" (Romans 8:31)
36. "We pray you in Christ's ____, be ye reconciled to God" (2 Corinthians 5:20)
37. "They wandered in deserts, and in mountains, and in ____" (Hebrews 11:38)
39. ____ of the Chaldees
40. Late actor Ames
42. Survived in water
47. Kind of scale
48. "Ye ____ bought with a price" (1 Corinthians 6:20)
49. Tabu, to toddler
50. Greek letter (pl.)
51. Nothing
52. Oaf; bully
53. Black, for one
54. Kind of glass
55. Sea bird

DOWN

1. "The gathering together of the waters called he ____" (Genesis 1:10)
2. "The devil threw him down and ____ him" (Luke 9:42)
3. "The churches of ____ salute you" (1 Corinthians 16:19)
4. "Produce your cause...bring forth your strong ____, saith the King of Jacob" (Isaiah 41:21)
5. There's partner
6. Sunday entree
7. "____ not I, but Christ liveth in me" (Galatians 2:20)
8. "The Lord is not ____ concerning his promise" (2 Peter 3:9)
9. Every
10. Soggy ground
11. Anger
19. "____ no man any thing, but to love" (Romans 13:8)
20. King of Judah; son of Abijam
23. Exclamation of delight
24. Earth
25. When this many are gathered together, the Lord is present
26. Christians worship the ____ true God
28. "A word spoken in ____ season, how good is it" (Proverbs 15:23)
29. Historical period
30. Unite

32. "How shall we sing the Lord's song in a ____ land?" (Psalm 137:4)
34. ___-oni, Rachel's youngest
35. Printer's measure
36. "A Boy Named ____" (J. Cash hit)
37. KJV verb
38. Airport runway
40. Recently, with "of"
41. Showing no favoritism (Fr.)
43. Call on for help
44. "Behold, I stand at the ____" (Revelation 3:20)
45. ____ Church, Virginia (site of 1864 battle)
46. Well ____
47. *Charlotte's* ____ (E.B. White classic)
48. Reply (abbr.)

PUZZLE 34

ACROSS

1. "Call me not Naomi, call me ____" (Ruth 1:20)
5. Bunch of bubbles
9. Paramedic's report (abbr.)
12. "The slaughter of Midian at the rock of ____" (Isaiah 10:26)
13. "Every ____ word that men shall speak, they shall give account" (Matthew 12:36)
14. There's the ___
15. "She...began to ____ his feet with tears" (Luke 7:38)
16. Burden
17. Compass dir.
18. "Let us build us a city and ____, whose top may reach unto heaven" (Genesis 11:4)
20. Lets off fumes
22. Ship to ___
24. Team _____, Olympics competitor
25. Attitude
26. Has ___
29. "It shall be even given thee to the ____ of the kingdom" (Esther 5:3)
33. Creative concept
35. "I will send a ____ , saying, Go, find the arrows" (1 Samuel 20:21)
36. Golden calf, for one
37. More is ___
38. Telegram word
40. United
41. Ram's mate
43. Captured, in a way
45. Lion's portion
48. "What is the chaff to the ___?" (Jeremiah 23:28)
50. Require effort
51. "He himself stayed in ____ for a season" (Acts 19:22)
53. Become bored
56. Linking verb
57. ____ stop
58. "Whatsoever shall be given you in that ____, that speak ye" (Mark 13:11)
59. Affirmative
60. Overeat, almost
61. Dagger

DOWN

1. Weekend job, for many
2. Son of Jether (1 Chronicles 7:38)
3. Gives new life, as the Lord
4. "Him shall the people curse, nations shall ____ him" (Proverbs 24:24)
5. Rank's partner
6. Scent
7. In the manner of
8. "Thy kingdom is divided, and given to the ____ and the Persians" (Daniel 5:28)
9. Three (Ger.)
10. Fire
11. Fortas and others
19. Where one surfs
21. Mother, hello (abbr.)
22. "Strengthen their mast, they could not spread the ____" (Isaiah 33:23)
23. "____ us from the face of him that sitteth on the throne" (Revelation 6:16)
24. Cancel; annul
27. In addition

28. Partake
30. "Ye have received the Spirit of ____, whereby we cry, Abba, Father" (Romans 8:15)
31. Single
32. "Then all the disciples forsook him, and ____" (Matthew 26:56)
34. Tribe of Israel (var.)
39. ____millennialism
42. Becomes useless, with "out"
44. Vows
45. "None can ____ his hand" (Daniel 4:35)
46. Unclean animal (Leviticus 11:6)
47. Cutting tools
48. Knew; learned (arch.)
49. "____ the evil" (Amos 5:15)
52. Aegean, for one
54. Regret
55. Poetic contraction

PUZZLE 35

ACROSS

1. Woolly ones
5. Under the weather
8. Mull over
12. Imply
13. Feminine Israeli name
14. Covenant
15. Make null
16. Attila, for one
17. Zone
18. "As newborn babes, ____ the sincere milk of the word" (1 Peter 2:2)
20. "____ is all, and in all" (Colossians 3:11)
22. Cable, for one
23. Hairpin curve
24. "In thy fear will I ____ toward thy holy temple" (Psalm 5:7)
28. Temporary dwellings
32. "For Adam was first formed, then ____" (1 Timothy 2:13)
33. Gratuity
35. Vowel trio
36. "To be a reproach and a proverb, a ____ and a curse" (Jeremiah 24:9)
39. "The dragon shalt thou ____ under feet" (Psalm 91:13)
42. ____ drum
44. "Ye ____ of your father the devil" (John 8:44)
45. Graven image, perhaps
48. Mental pictures
52. Hope
53. Donkey
55. Disreputable establishment
56. Sheltered side
57. "A faithful witness will not ____" (Proverbs 14:5)
58. Appliance
59. "The day of the Lord is ____" (Joel 3:14)
60. Sra, in Sarasota
61. Left

DOWN

1. Son of Gera, the second judge of Israel (Judges 3:15)
2. "Woe to them that are mighty to drink ____" (Isaiah 5:22)
3. "The Creator of the ____ of the earth, fainteth not" (Isaiah 40:28)
4. Group of philosophers who met Paul at Athens (Acts 17:18)
5. "They that do such things shall not ____ the kingdom of God" (Galatians 5:21)
6. President Hoover's wife, familiarly
7. Masculine name
8. Rough; earthy
9. Mata ____
10. Summers, in Nice
11. Reporter's question
19. Stadium sound
21. Honolulu's time zone
24. ____ paint
25. Eggs
26. Father of Serug (Genesis 11:20)
27. "To him was given the key of the bottomless ____" (Revelation 9:1)
29. Snooze
30. Up to that point (var.)
31. Feminine nickname
34. The children of the Proverbs 31 woman call her blessed, and the husband ____ her
37. "They are all delivered unto death, to the ____ parts of the earth" (Ezekiel 31:14)

38. Greek letter
40. "The isles shall wait upon me, and on mine ____ shall they trust" (Isaiah 51:5)
41. Bucolic spot
43. King's bailiwick
45. ____ song
46. Mosaic piece
47. On a steamer
49. "____ unto the Lord the glory due unto his name" (Psalm 96:8)
50. Tied
51. Dispatched
54. Title of respect

PUZZLE 36

ACROSS

1. Cleo's killer
4. Asa or Ahab
8. Perfect
12. "They cast ____, that is, the lot, before Haman" (Esther 3:7)
13. One who sold his birthright
14. "As he saith also in ____, I will call them my people" (Romans 9:25)
15. Where one uses a wood
16. "Six ____ shalt thou labour and do all thy work" (Exodus 20:9)
17. Reporter's question
18. "There shall come a ____ out of Jacob and a Sceptre shall rise" (Numbers 24:17)
20. Word's partner
21. "Stretch out the ____ that is in thy hand toward Ai" (Joshua 8:18)
23. Greek letter
25. To exhibit exhaustion
26. Burdened one
27. Golden State (abbr.)
29. Godfrey, to friends
30. "The word is nigh thee, even in thy mouth, and in thy ____" (Romans 10:8)
31. "For the Father...hath committed all judgment unto the ____" (John 5:22)
32. Bible div.
33. "Ye shall be baptized with the Holy Ghost not many days ____" (Acts 1:5)
34. KJV verb
35. Out of (arch.)
36. Says "whoa"
37. "I am the ____ vine" (John 15:1)
38. "Nadab and Abihu...offered strange ____ before the Lord" (Leviticus 10:1)
39. Hurries
40. Speed
42. Compass dir.
45. Opposed to aweather
46. "In ____ there was a voice heard, lamentation" (Matthew 2:18)
47. Iowa college
48. Kind of hall
49. Memo part
50. Before

DOWN

1. "A bishop the must be...____ to teach" (1 Timothy 3:2)
2. Betty White role on "Mary Tyler Moore" TV show
3. "God is...a very ____ help in trouble" (Psalm 46:1)
4. "Arabia, and all the princes of ____...in these were thy merchants" (Ezekiel 27:21)
5. Danube tributary
6. Negative vote
7. Masculine nickname
8. American social reformer Julia
9. Son of Nun of the tribe of Ephraim (Numbers 13:8)
10. "I am instructed...both to abound and to suffer ____" (Philippians 4:12)
11. Poetic contraction
19. Make lace
20. KJV verb
21. Measure of length
22. Say adieu
23. "____ hither thy finger, and behold my hands" (John 20:27)

24. Tortoise's opponent
26. "My people are ____ to back sliding from me" (Hosea 11:7)
27. Pasture youngster
28. They head for the hills
30. Now's partner
31. "Let the lying lips be put to ____" (Psalm 31:18)
33. Provides shelter
34. "We do not ____ after the flesh" (2 Corinthians 10:3)
35. Loosens
36. "So ____ gave Solomon cedar trees and fir trees" (1 Kings 5:10)
37. Game piece
38. "His ____ went throughout all Syria" (Matthew 4:24)
39. Son of Noah
40. Every third (comb. form)
41. "____ thou not the bread of him that hath an evil eye" (Proverbs 23:6)
43. Conjunction
44. Shoe width

PUZZLE 37

ACROSS

1. Atlas and Apennines (abbr.)
4. "Is there no ____ in Gilead?" (Jeremiah 8:22)
8. Son of Omri; notoriously evil king
12. Gershwin
13. Great Lake
14. KJV verb
15. Complete collections
17. "Thou shalt not plow with an ox and an ____ together" (Deuteronomy 22:10)
18. Curtain or horse
19. Canines, for example
21. Stage direction
23. Legal object
25. Chemical suffix
26. Certain physician (abbr.)
28. "The yoke shall be destroyed because of the ____" (Isaiah 10:27)
32. ____ ear
33. "Whatsoever a man soweth, that shall he also ____" (Galatians 6:7)
34. Energy unit
35. Mad at
36. "They ____ my path, they set forward my calamity" (Job 30:13)
37. "There were set there six ____ of stone" (John 2:6)
39. Elder (abbr.)
40. "The everlasting ____, the Lord" (Isaiah 40:28)
41. One fleet of foot in the forest
42. Grand ____ auto
44. "Let them praise his name in the ____" (Psalm 149:3)
48. "____ went before the ark" (2 Samuel 6:4)
50. Linking verb
52. "____ my lips"
53. Works like a gem
54. Steadfast
56. KJV grain
57. Aid's partner
58. Saline drop
59. "When we came to the ____, that we opened our sacks" (Genesis 43:21)

DOWN

1. "There went up a ____ from the earth and watered" (Genesis 2:6)
2. Birch or ginkgo
3. Make contented
4. "____ it ever so humble..."
5. Son of Jether (1 Chronicles 7:38)
6. Feminine name
7. "A thorn in the flesh, the ____ of Satan" (2 Corinthians 12:7)
8. "____ in me, and I in you" (John 15:4)
9. Animal not to be eaten (Deuteronomy 14:7)
10. Hubbub
11. Actor Cross
16. Sunset, for one
20. Coop dowager
22. Participle suffix
24. Hardly fickle
26. Gossip, literally (colloq.)
27. Addition column
28. "God is thy refuge, and underneath are the everlasting ____" (Deuteronomy 33:27)
29. "Thou art ____, O Lord" (Psalm 119:151)
30. Paddle
31. NYC subway

32. "Is any thing ____ hard for the Lord?" (Genesis 18:14)
35. Asparagus unit
37. Sorrow
38. "The staff of his shoulder, the ____ of his oppressor" (Isaiah 9:4)
40. "The Holy ____ shall come upon thee" (Luke 1:35)
42. ____ and again
43. Colorfast
45. Father of Salathiel (Luke 3:27)
46. "Whosoever slayeth ____, vengeance shall be taken on him" (Genesis 4:15)
47. Idyllic spot
48. Exclamation
49. Where the action is
51. Baseball stat.
55. Son of Judah (1 Chronicles 2:3)

PUZZLE 38

ACROSS

1. Sign of the end times (Matthew 24:6)
5. "Fear God and ____ his commandments" (Ecclesiastes 12:13)
9. Trucker's "motel"
12. "He [Isaac] called the name of the well ____" (Genesis 26:20)
13. Exclamation
14. Tint
15. Sinks
17. "I was afraid, and went and hid thy ____" (Matthew 25:25)
19. ____ and the Thummin (Exodus 28:30)
20. "My servant ____ at home sick" (Matthew 8:6)
21. Puts an end to
23. Parts of capitols
25. Charade
26. In the near future (arch.)
28. "Buy the truth and ____ it not" (Proverbs 23:23)
31. Preposition
32. Church part (pl.)
34. That is (abbr.)
35. "Ye may rejoice, and that I may be the ____ sorrowful" (Philippians 2:28)
38. Nuisance
39. Promise Keepers attendees
40. "Ye shall receive ____, after that the Holy Ghost is come" (Acts 1:8)
42. "____ your ways and your doings" (Jeremiah 7:3)
44. "There ____ from heaven a great light" (Acts 22:6)
46. Actor Thicke
47. Unleashed
49. "Those who by reason of use have their ____ exercised to discern" (Hebrews 5:14)
52. Holiday, for one
53. Choose's cohort
55. Settle in a cozy spot
56. French pronoun
57. "Thou hadst cast me...in the midst of the ____" (Jonah 2:3)
58. "The poison of ____ is under their lips" (Romans 3:13)

DOWN

1. Entanglement
2. Good king of Judah
3. Consequence
4. Avoid
5. Abyssinian weight
6. Chicago transport (abbr.)
7. "In the day you ____ thereof, then your eyes shall be opened" (Genesis 3:5)
8. "Sing unto the Lord with...the voice of a ____" (Psalm 98:5)
9. "Hast thou not...curdled me like ____" (Job 10:10)
10. Orpah, to Obed
11. House, in Hebrew
16. Hebrew month
18. "Behold, thou [Samson] hast mocked me [Delilah], and told me ____" (Judges 16:10)
21. Greet
22. Teen trauma
23. Capital of Delaware
24. Singles
27. Back of the neck
29. Property claim
30. Let borrow
33. Not fresh

36. Forks' cohorts
37. "As my beloved ____ I warn you" (1 Corinthians 4:14)
39. Monthly occurrence
41. Mourns
43. "Our fathers did eat ____ in the desert" (John 6:31)
44. Skirt feature
45. Practice and practice and practice
46. Queries
48. "To live is Christ and to ____ is gain" (Philippians 1:21)
50. Extra sense (abbr.)
51. Byways (abbr.)
54. About (abbr.)

PUZZLE 39

ACROSS

1. Buys (tickets) for later profit
7. "Believe on the Lord Jesus Christ, and thou shalt be ____" (Acts 16:31)
12. "An inheritance may be gotten ____ at the beginning" (Proverbs 20:21)
14. John, on Patmos
15. Luc, to Lisette
16. Kind of shot or shirt
17. Napa Valley sight (pl.)
18. Depilatory brand
20. "The ____ of sin is death" (Romans 6:23)
22. Note on the diatonic scale
23. Mete out
25. Bleed, as madras
26. Body of water (Fr.)
27. "Lo, I see four men ____, walking in the midst of the fire" (Daniel 3:25)
29. Horse hair
30. Aircraft authority
32. "Remember how ____ my time is" (Psalm 89:47)
34. 1/1000 of an inch (pl.)
35. Has strong feelings about
37. Ocean (abbr.)
38. Solidify
39. "Who hath...____ out heaven with the span" (Isaiah 40:12)
43. Borders VA and MD
44. Sewing fundamentals
46. "____ thyself, and come down from the cross" (Mark 15:30)
47. Interjection
48. Conjunction
49. Shoe size
51. Sue ____, honey brand
52. Traversed by *les bateaux mouches*
54. RSVP request
56. Ash and aspen
57. Wears; dons

DOWN

1. Columnist Alexander
2. "It is easier for a ____ to go through the eye of a needle" (Matthew 19:24)
3. Father of Seraiah (1 Chronicles 4:35)
4. Army officer (abbr.)
5. Pothole's cousin
6. Whole bunch
7. "I will serve thee ____ years for Rachel" (Genesis 29:18)
8. Alignment between countries
9. French export, to the French
10. Earth or air, for example
11. "Master...do for us whatsoever we shall ____" (Mark 10:35)
13. "Receive my sayings; and the ____ of thy life shall be many" (Proverbs 4:10)
19. Road trip expenses, sometimes
21. "That he was gone to be ____ with a man that is a sinner" (Luke 19:7)
24. As well
26. "Neither shalt thou ____ the corners of thy beard" (Leviticus 19:27)
28. Further; additional
29. Husband of Zipporah
30. He doesn't want to be called for a balk
31. "Love worketh no ____ to his neighbour" (Romans 13:10)
33. Haw's partner
34. "Thou ____ him a little lower than the angels" (Hebrews 2:7)

36. Change
38. Stations (Fr.)
40. Bible mount near Nazareth
41. Occurrence
42. "Ye have put off the old man with his ____" (Colossians 3:9)
44. Exhausted, with "in"
45. Understands
50. Particularly (abbr.)
53. Common abbr.
55. River in Italy

PUZZLE 40

ACROSS

1. Revolutionary hero Nathan
5. Step made by faith
9. Age of Methuselah when he had a son: one hundred eighty-____ (Genesis 5:25)
10. Aerie dweller
12. This may include "or else"
13. Most faithful
15. "There stood before the river a ____ which had two horns" (Daniel 8:3)
16. Treasured, in a way
18. Assess
19. Herdsman of Tekoia whom God called to be a prophet
21. Rod and ____
23. Bishopric
24. Noted Quaker family, and others
26. Chooses
28. At odds (abbr.)
30. Songdom's "gal"
31. "The way of man is ____ and strange" (Proverbs 21:8)
35. Is diminished
39. "Go, sell the ____, and pay thy debt" (2 Kings 4:7)
40. He went searching for his father's lost donkeys
42. Neap, for one
43. "Incline not my heart to any ____ thing" (Psalm 141:4)
45. Sesquicentennial segment
47. Mature
48. Stern
50. Like-_____ (kindred spirit)
52. "The angels shall...____ the wicked from among the just" (Matthew 13:49)
53. Ezekiel saw a valley that was full of ___
54. Takes no action
55. "There shall come forth a rod out of the ____ of Jesse" (Isaiah 11:1)

DOWN

1. Mount on the northeastern boundary of Palestine (Joshua 12:1)
2. Roadway (abbr.)
3. Seep
4. Door direction
5. Colossians and Philippians, familiarly
6. What one lends
7. "The words of ___the son of Jakeh, even the prophecy" (Proverbs 30:1)
8. "Do I seek to ____ men?" (Galatians 1:10)
9. "Let them be confounded and put to ____" (Psalm 35:4)
11. Fragrant compound
12. Sand, for one
14. Wooden pegs
17. Vitality
20. Twentieth-century English novelist
22. "His ____ also shall not wither" (Psalm 1:3)
25. LaCosta, and others
27. Apartment
29. "He had offered up ____ and supplications with strong crying" (Hebrews 5:7)
31. Those opposed
32. Splits
33. Mount of ___
34. ____ date
36. "Thou shalt also be...a royal ____ in the hand of thy God" (Isaiah 62:3)

37. "These things, saith he which hath the sharp sword with two ____" (Revelation 2:12)
38. ____ money
41. "Two ____ of the first year for a sacrifice of peace" (Leviticus 23:19)
44. Israel's high priest had to descend from this tribe
46. Lose control
49. Soak flax
51. Compass dir.

PUZZLE 41

ACROSS

1. Cartographer's creation
4. Had a stroke
8. Captain Hook's henchman
12. Mother of Hezekiah (2 Kings 18:2)
13. "The king arose, and ____ his garments" (2 Samuel 13:31)
14. "I ____ you!"
15. "My money is ___; and lo, it is even in my sack" (Genesis 42:28)
17. Deserve
18. Mar, in a way
19. "Beware of the scribes, which love...the chief ____ in the synagogues" (Mark 12:38,39)
21. English breakfast, for one
23. Keeps away from
26. Cathedral feature
29. "The vine languisheth, all the merry hearted do ____" (Isaiah 24:7)
32. Norma ____ (Sally Field role)
33. "He that hath clean hands and a ____ heart" (Psalm 24:4)
34. Worldwide workers group (abbr.)
35. Fantasy (Fr.)
36. Time for *les grandes vacances*
37. College building
38. "Thou hast been in ____ the garden of God" (Ezekiel 28:13)
39. "Evening ____" (former TV show)
41. Part of a circle (abbr.)
43. Tithe fraction
46. Park ____ (neighborhood in Brooklyn, NY)
50. ____ Canal
52. "____ his marvellous works...his wonders" (1 Chronicles 16:12)
54. Circuit
55. Mouths
56. On; upon (prefix)
57. ____ room
58. Blemish
59. Actress Sandra

DOWN

1. ____ Hill, where Paul spoke in Athens
2. Assist
3. City on the Arno River
4. "The ____ that smote the image became a great mountain" (Daniel 2:35)
5. "The words of his mouth were smoother than butter, but ____ was in his heart" (Psalm 55:21)
6. Mythological god of war
7. Babylonian conqueror
8. "Smite...and destroy all the children of ____" (Numbers 24:17)
9. "The children of Israel...cannot be ____ nor numbered" (Hosea 1:10)
10. "Men have not heard, nor perceived by the ____" (Isaiah 64:4)
11. Sea bird
16. "Ye pay ____ of mint and anise" (Matthew 23:23)
20. Furniture wood
22. "They...were forbidden of the Holy Ghost to preach the word in ____" (Acts 16:6)
24. Church part
25. Observed
26. Mirrors
27. Orpah's sister-in-law
28. "From the beginning of the ____ God made them male and female" (Mark 10:6)

30. ____ at ease
31. "They should not worship devils and idols of ____" (Revelation 9:20)
35. King's domain
37. Little red one
40. "Thou hast laid me in the lowest pit...in the ____" (Psalm 88:6)
42. To cause to be (suffix, Brit.)
44. "Doth he thank that servant...? I ____ not" (Luke 17:9)
45. Wife of Zeus
47. Grandfather of David
48. Cartoon character LePew
49. Pennsylvania city
50. Small-town America street
51. ____ v. Wade
53. "They ____ my path, they set forward my calamity" (Job 30:13)

PUZZLE 42

ACROSS

1. Wrath
4. Send out
8. "They made a calf...and offered sacrifice unto the ____" (Acts 7:41)
12. From or to a distance (prefix)
13. "He maketh the storm a ____" (Psalm 107:29)
14. Bog
15. He thought Hannah had been drinking
16. Bold alternative
17. Disobey a road sign
18. "Do good to them that ____ you" (Matthew 5:44)
20. Lady of Spain, perhaps (abbr.)
21. "In thee, O Lord, do I put my ____" (Psalm 71:1)
23. "____ God in the day of visitation" (1 Peter 2:12)
27. Clarifying abbr.
28. From here one has a bird's-eye view
30. Ripped apart (arch.)
31. Feminine name
33. "There is a ____, the streams whereof shall make glad" (Psalm 46:4)
35. Little lamb's cry
36. Land measure
38. AKA Cephas
40. Title of respect (abbr.)
41. What Demetrius the silversmith made (Acts 19:24)
43. Children of the vindicated Job: ____ sons and three daughters
44. Number of pieces of silver belonging to the woman in the parable of the lost coin
45. Cash cow (abbr.)
46. Isle of ____, in the English Channel
49. Arafat's assoc.
50. Not a lot
53. Buffalo's lake
54. ____ *Window* (Hitchcock film)
55. Before
56. Coffin
57. "____ it even to the foundation thereof" (Psalm 137:7)
58. Tribe of Israel

DOWN

1. Believer in (suffix)
2. Cousin, e.g.
3. U.S. statesman Root
4. "I will ____ you abroad among the nations" (Nethemiah 1:8)
5. Actor Alan
6. "They angered him... so that it went ____ with Moses" (Psalm 106:32)
7. Britain's John Major, once (abbr.)
8. "That I may ____ unto you some spiritual gift" (Romans 1:11)
9. "I must ____ in this land" (Deuteronomy 4:22)
10. Mine find
11. What Fred Astaire did?
17. Hit's inits.
19. Good king of Judah
20. Storm hazard
21. Son of Japheth (Genesis 10:2)
22. Toothbrush brand
23. "What ___?"
24. The Great ____ ____ (name for God)
25. "For he knoweth our ___; he remembereth that we are dust" (Psalm 103:14)

26. Pine
29. What sour grapes do, hopefully
32. To blunder
34. "I will ____ health unto thee" (Jeremiah 30:17)
37. One or the other
39. Jerky movement during sleep (abbr.)
42. "I will spread my ____ upon them" (Hosea 7:12)
45. Exclamation of pity
46. Sticky trap
47. Son of Bela (1 Chronicles 7:7)
48. Give (Scot.)
49. Legume
50. "I have ____ you with milk" (1 Corinthians 3:2)
51. Tide competitor
52. Benign skin tumor
54. B & O, e.g.

PUZZLE 43

ACROSS

1. "The ____ trees of the wheels were joined to the base" (1 Kings 7:32)
5. Ingredient in some cereals
9. Father of Kish (1 Samuel 9:1)
10. "____ up a child in the way he should go" (Proverbs 22:6)
12. Achieve success (colloq.)
13. "Mount Sion, which is ____" (Deuteronomy 4:48)
15. Fuss
16. Let go, not so nicely
18. Greek letter
19. Utility org. for noncity dwellers
20. Main rooms of ancient Roman house
22. Poetic contraction
23. Support one's alma mater
25. Job requirements
27. Stack or rack
29. "Ye shall go out with joy and be ____ forth with peace" (Isaiah 55:12)
30. Side and back, to name two
34. Narrow, deep pass
38. The style of (suffix)
39. Accustomed oneself, with "into"
41. Son of Benjamin (Genesis 46:21)
42. Push, and even shove
43. Inhabitant, e.g. (abbr.)
44. "Ye shall be hated of all ____" (Matthew 10:22)
45. Hope for all generations: Jesus has ____ from the dead!
48. Saturated with liquid, with "up"
51. "Laying up in ____ for themselves a good foundation" (1 Timothy 6:19)
52. "For we which have believed do ____ into rest" (Hebrews 4:3)
53. Taken to court
54. "Call ye upon him while he is ____" (Isaiah 55:6)

DOWN

1. Europe, in particular, to Americans
2. Hours in the day, to a centurion
3. O.T. book
4. "For Jacob my servant's sake, and Israel mine ____" (Isaiah 45:4)
5. Brother of Caleb (Joshua 15:17)
6. Linking verb
7. Black liquid
8. Tribe of Israel
9. Actress Eve
11. "But I will shew thee that which is ____ in the scripture" (Daniel 10:21)
12. River in Switzerland
14. Fashion designer Byron
17. Son of Benjamin (Genesis 46:21)
20. "Now it is high time to ____... now is our salvation nearer" (Romans 13:11)
21. "____ you ways and your doings" (Jeremiah 7:3)
24. Exclamation of surprise
26. Fuss
28. Ached
30. Watery animal fluid (pl.)
31. Alexander and others
32. Forgives; pardons
33. Compass dir.
35. "The third part of an hin of oil to ____ with the fine flour" (Ezekiel 46:14)
36. "Be of good ___; I have overcome the world" (John 16:33)

37. "Naphtali is a ____ let loose" (Genesis 49:21)
40. Industrial center in Germany
46. French coin
47. Before
49. "As the body is ____, and hath many members" (1 Corinthians 12:12)
50. School org.

PUZZLE 44

ACROSS

1. Sinful
4. "And the Spirit and the ____ say, Come" (Revelation 22:17)
9. Word in many ranch names
12. On the outside (prefix)
13. To let slacken
14. Put on ____ (postpone)
15. Rebelled against
17. Convalesced
19. Friendly and Flintstone
21. "Shall I come unto you with a ____, or in love" (1 Corinthians 4:21)
22. "I give unto you power to ____ on serpents" (Luke 10:19)
24. "The labour of the righteous ____ to life" (Proverbs 10:16)
28. Actor William
29. Ms. Moreno
30. "As it was in the days of ____" (Luke 17:26)
31. Product safety inits.
32. "There was a rainbow...in sight like unto an ____" (Revelation 4:3)
35. Western state (abbr.)
36. NYC opera house
38. "Ye shall eat neither bread nor parched corn, nor green ____" (Leviticus 23:14)
39. Protest
41. Kind of alphabet
43. Dispatches
44. Requirement for college (abbr.)
45. Provides sketchy information
47. Spice rack spice
50. Like a mule, supposedly
53. Miner's pay dirt
54. "Neither let us ____ Christ, as some of them" (1 Corinthians 10:9)
56. Actor Louis
57. ____ & breakfast
58. "Foxes have ____" (Luke 9:58)
59. Oolong, for one

DOWN

1. "I remember thee upon my ____" (Psalm 63:6)
2. Mirror
3. "Who maketh thee to ____ from another?" (1 Corinthians 4:7)
4. To be fruitful
5. Comedian Foxx
6. Within; toward (prefix)
7. "Mine eye also is ____ by reason of sorrow" (Job 17:7)
8. "The ____ God is thy refuge" (Deuteronomy 33:27)
9. Implored (arch.)
10. Team's "winningest" pitcher
11. ____ Sea
16. Consumed with anger
18. Where Cain dwelled: land of ___
20. "I was dumb with silence...and my sorrow was ____" (Psalm 39:2)
22. Tom of Ringling Bros. fame
23. "I will make thee ____ over many things" (Matthew 25:21)
25. Greek letters
26. Namely (2 words)
27. Gives new life, as Jesus Christ does
29. Camino ___
33. "My soul ____ for heaviness" (Psalm 119:28)

34. "They that will be rich fall...into many...lusts, which ____ men in destruction" (1 Timothy 6:9)
37. "When the ruler of the feast had ____ the water that was made wine" (John 2:9)
40. Say okay
42. "____ ____ [2 words] with you, saith the Lord" (Haggai 1:13)
43. Book divisions
46. On cowboy's saddle checklist
47. ____ Hill, San Francisco
48. Office or function (suffix)
49. Neon competitor
51. Grain
52. KJV assent
55. Metric measure (abbr.)

PUZZLE 45

ACROSS

1. Horned mammal, often mentioned in the Bible
4. Son of (Hebrew)
7. ____ of Man
10. Tizzy
11. Compass pt.
12. One from Tarsus
14. "The younger son...____ his substance with riotous living" (Luke 15:13)
16. "Aaron and ____ stayed up his hands" (Exodus 17:12)
17. Exclamation of relief
19. Many moons
20. Mother ___
21. Jeanne d'Arc, for one (abbr.)
22. Hive dweller
24. "Exalt him that is ____" (Ezekiel 21:26)
25. To dam up
26. Simile syntax
27. "____ thou on my right hand" (Mark 12:36)
28. Legume
29. ____ eagle (skating stunt)
32. Almost
35. Cereal grain
36. Baseball great Drysdale
37. That is (abbr.)
38. "What do ye, loosing the ____" (Mark 11:5)
40. "Ye are grown ____ as the heifer at grass" (Jeremiah 50:11)
41. Appeal
43. Hole-making device
44. Put down
45. Nemesis, certainly
46. Exist
47. Outward appearance
48. "Do I seek to ___men?" (Galatians 1:10)
51. "____ thyself now with majesty and excellency" (Job 40:10)
53. ____ Dolorosa
54. "All the rivers ____ unto the sea" (Ecclesiastes 1:7)
55. Consumed
56. "Go to the ____, thou sluggard" (Proverbs 6:6)
57. Mamie Eisenhower, ____ Dowd

DOWN

1. Unrefined
2. Michigan town near Grand Rapids
3. Brother of Miriam
4. Has ___
5. Kind of game
6. Quadrant in D.C.
7. "All the women...in wisdom ____ goats' hair" (Exodus 35:26)
8. Paddle
9. Greek letter
13. Better than never
15. Big ___: circus site
16. "____ thee two tables of stone" (Exodus 34:1)
18. It gets let down
20. Kind of plate
21. "We have seen his ____ in the east" (Matthew 2:2)
22. "And there ____ light" (Genesis 1:3)
23. Slithering one
24. Put a ____ on it
25. Galilee, for one
27. Made a lap
28. Do a scribe's work

30. Bagel's basic kin
31. "And he said unto me, Take it, and ____ it up" (Revelation 10:9)
32. Slangy negative
33. "I speak the truth in Christ and ____ not" (1 Timothy 2:7)
34. Yes, to King James
36. "The ____ of the Lord is at hand" (Joel 1:15)
38. NYC sight
39. "One ____ five hundred pence, and the other fifty" (Luke 7:41)
40. ____ East
41. "Annabel Lee" poet
42. "Go ye and ____ what that meaneth" (Matthew 9:13)
44. Word in Valley Girl's vocabulary
45. Slipper, for example
47. Form of legislation
48. Bobby, for one
49. Feminine nickname
50. Compass pt.
52. Apiece (abbr.)
53. One of the thirteen colonies (abbr.)

PUZZLE 46

ACROSS

1. ____ Colonies, in eastern Iowa
6. Balmy weekend sky sight (pl.)
11. "I will bring the third part through the fire and will ____ them" (Zechariah 13:9)
13. Reason for saying "excuse me"
14. Popular NYC art museum, for short
15. Org. that includes Braves but not Indians
16. Pacific state (abbr.)
17. Pitcher's stat.
18. Mulberry, for one (abbr.)
19. Recover from the attic? (2 words)
22. Masculine nickname
23. "And ____ were the more added to the Lord" (Acts 5:14)
25. Prohibits
27. Compass pt.
28. Site of Miami University
31. Door sign
32. "Open ___"
33. Pictured on highway sign
34. Sporty Ford model
37. Mimic
38. "Ye became ____ of us and of the Lord" (1 Thessalonians 1:6)
41. Hospital abbr.
43. Desired deeply
44. Kind of M.D.
46. Bygone automobile
48. Article
49. Sound of hesitation
50. Library section (abbr.)
51. "Thou shalt heap coals of fire upon his head, and the Lord shall ____ thee" (Proverbs 25:22)
53. Missouri and Ohio
55. Mohair measure
56. "The way of an ____ in the air" (Proverbs 30:19)

DOWN

1. "Underneath are the everlasting ____" (Deuteronomy 33:27)
2. Track competition
3. Astern
4. Metal in a 5-ct. piece
5. Abolish
6. Butter, for one
7. Common abbr.
8. Summer wear, for short
9. Old Testament scribe
10. "____ the law among my disciples" (Isaiah 8:16)
12. Feminine nickname
13. More pointed than push
19. "There is one lawgiver, who is able to save and to ____" (James 4:12)
20. "Abram had dwelt ____ years in the land" (Genesis 16:3)
21. "A ____ man soweth strife" (Proverbs 16:28)
23. Lawyer's homework
24. "King Solomon made a navy of ____" (1 Kings 9:26)
25. "Arise, take up thy ____, and go" (Matthew 9:6)
26. Let go (colloq.)
29. Chemical suffix
30. Poetic contraction
34. Pituitary, for one
35. Rocky hill
36. Land ____
39. "Now ____ a parable of the fig tree" (Matthew 24:32)
40. Strange
41. Answers incorrectly

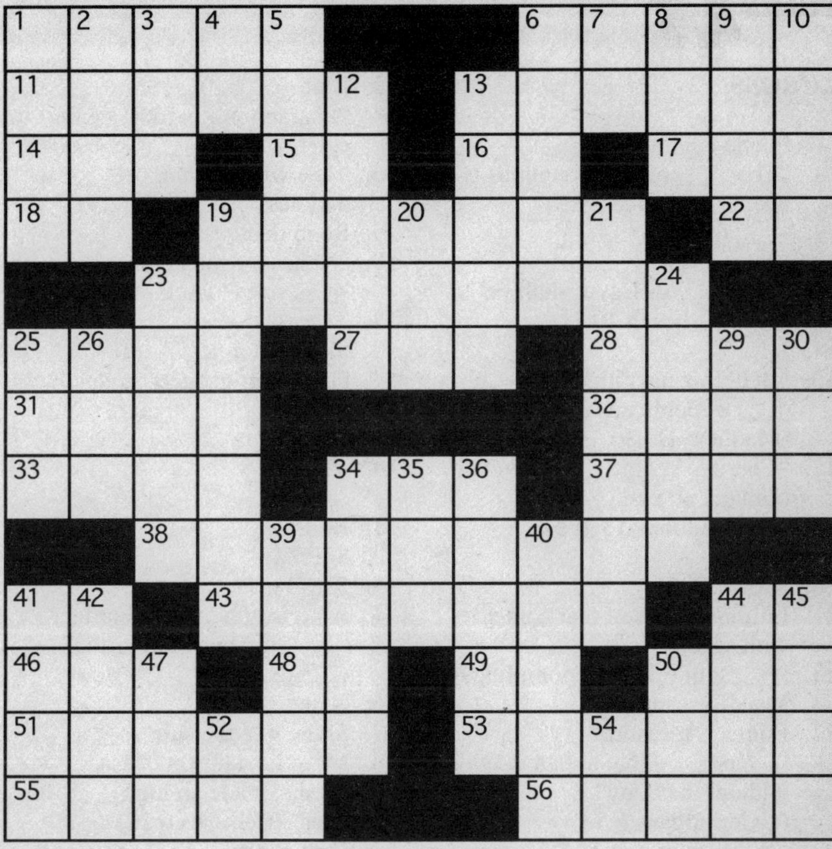

42. Exude fumes
44. "That ____" (one-time TV sitcom)
45. Assume a position
47. Assume a mortgage, for example
50. "Let his children be continually vagabonds, and ____" (Psalm 109:10)
52. "I have given into thy hand the king of ____" (Joshua 8:1)
54. Site of Jamestown (abbr.)

PUZZLE 47

ACROSS

1. Poetic contraction
4. "The ____ of the mountains is his pasture" (Job 39:8)
9. ____ fried
12. Linking verb
13. "The ____ of Egypt shall be moved" (Isaiah 19:1)
14. Inlet
15. "Behold a man gluttonous...a ____ of publicans and sinners" (Matthew 11:19)
17. "Charity...is not ____ provoked, thinketh no evil" (1 Corinthians 13:4, 5)
19. Joke
20. Brownish gray
21. Liturgical season that coincides with spring
23. ____ sum (Chinese dumplings)
24. Man, for example
27. Printer's measures
28. "Every ____ that a man doeth is without the body" (1 Corinthians 6:18)
29. "When thou prayest, ____ into thy closet" (Matthew 6:6)
30. ____ out (tennis term)
31. "The ____ went before, the players on instruments followed" (Psalm 68:25)
33. Movie rating
34. "Pay that which thou hast ____" (Ecclesiastes 5:4)
36. Singing syllable
37. About
38. Pitcher
39. James Herriot, for short
40. Driven group
41. "But ____ foolish questions, and genealogies" (Titus 3:9)
43. Blue
44. "Pharaoh was wroth...against the chief of the ____" (Genesis 40:2)
46. "The wicked shall be ____ in darkness" (1 Samuel 2:9)
49. Be in debt
50. "Aeneas, which had kept his bed ____ years" (Acts 9:33)
52. Years and years
53. Skin tumor
54. Grown-up gadgets, collectively
55. Ran into

DOWN

1. Boor
2. Stumble
3. Royal eras
4. American humorist Lardner
5. "____ to your faith virtue" (2 Peter 1:5)
6. Negative
7. Shine like the sun
8. More hirsute son of Isaac
9. "Jesus, made an high ____ for ever" (Hebrews 6:20)
10. Fare poorly
11. Negative, old style
16. Sup
18. Twirls
20. Got goosebumps
21. Make a getaway
22. "He shall surely ____ her to be his wife" (Exodus 22:16)
23. Noise level
25. Disdained individual, in Bible times
26. Energy unit
28. Caesar
29. TV series
31. "If any man ____ me, let him follow me" (John 12:26)

32. "Where wilt thou that we prepare for thee to ____ the passover?" (Matthew 26:17)
35. "O Lucifer...which didst ____ the nations" (Isaiah 14:12)
37. "I will ____ them from death" (Hosea 13:14)
39. Call on
40. Masculine nickname
42. Swedish coin
43. Tends to tots, tersely
44. Half a canine call
45. Reverence
46. Less than, with "of"
47. "As it was in the days of ____" (Luke 17:26)
48. Terminator, in a way (abbr.)
51. Matthew 28:19 verb

PUZZLE 48

ACROSS

1. "And falling into a place where two ____ met, they ran the ship aground" (Acts 27:41)
5. Father of Adoniram (1 Kings 4:6)
9. Linking verb
12. Yen
13. "I will fasten him as a ____ in a sure place" (Isaiah 22:23)
14. "La ____" (Debussy composition)
15. Tear
16. "And David saith, Let their table be made a...____" (Romans 11:9)
17. Certain vegetable serving
18. Extraordinary, in a way
20. "She layeth her ____ to the spindle" (Proverbs 31:19)
22. "If ye be reproached for the name of Christ, ____ are ye" (1 Peter 4:14)
24. Flap
25. Like a New York minute (abbr.)
26. At ___
29. Watch ___
33. Is supine
35. Cotton ___
36. Genus of the lily family
37. "My father did ____ you with a heavy yoke" (1 Kings 12:11)
38. Remove bobby pins
40. ____ the line
41. Poetic before
43. Rethink and revise
45. "He will not always _____: neither will he keep his anger" (Psalm 103:9)
48. It's sometimes glaring
50. "Thy word have I ____ in mine heart" (Psalm 119:11)
51. Kind of light or line
53. Tribe of Israel
56. Natural combination of minerals
57. Kilmer subject
58. And others (abbr.)
59. Pod dweller
60. "O ____ out thy light and thy truth" (Psalm 43:3)
61. Synagogue

DOWN

1. Polite title
2. Greek letter
3. "Behold, now is the ____ time; behold, now is the day of salvation" (2 Corinthians 6:2)
4. "We thy people and ____ of thy pasture" (Psalm 79:13)
5. Kind of hero
6. "John ____ witness of him" (John 1:15)
7. Circle part (abbr.)
8. Wave or ray
9. So be it
10. "They could not ____ the writing" (Daniel 5:8)
11. Solomon writes that whoever refuses reproof ___
19. Pastrami on ____ (deli order)
21. "____ Father, all things are possible" (Mark 14:36)
22. "I...have the keys of ____ and of death" (Revelation 1:18)
23. Continent
24. Mind the store
27. Marked by chills
28. "Where ____ abounded, grace did much more" (Romans 5:20)
30. "The law of the Medes and Persians, which ____ not" (Daniel 6:8)
31. High time

32. "A prophet mighty in ____ and word" (Luke 24:19)
34. Kind of money
39. Boathouse sight
42. Musical notations
44. Underground workers
45. Kind of house
46. "The labourer is worthy of his ____" (Luke 10:7)
47. Notion
48. "All the trees of ____, the choice and best of Lebanon" (Ezekiel 31:16)
49. "A bruised ____ shall he not break" (Matthew 12:20)
52. Wrath
54. Hebrew letter
55. Under the weather

PUZZLE 49

ACROSS

1. "What ____ I am afraid, I will trust in thee" (Psalm 56:3)
5. "They cast ____, that is, the lot, before Haman" (Esther 3:7)
8. It's not exactly red
12. In the near future (arch.)
13. Gobbled up
14. First two words in Key's composition
15. "Help thou mine ____" (Mark 9:24)
17. *Au* ____ (teenaged helper)
18. Relieve
19. Filled with evil desires, as a heart
21. Synonym for scow
24. Toward the sheltered side
25. "____ them that have the rule over you" (Hebrews 13:17)
26. "Thou hast ____ me when I was in distress" (Psalm 4:1)
30. Legal object
31. Michael, for one
32. Poem
33. "Yea, I ____ unto you, and... none of you that convinced Job" (Job 32:12)
35. Zone
36. Beverages
37. Squander
38. Cyrus was the king of ____ (Ezra 3:7)
41. One who hisses
42. Skirt feature
43. "Be sober, be ____" (1 Peter 5:8)
48. Melita, for one
49. Natural mineral
50. Day before (pl.)
51. Samuel, to some
52. See ___
53. Want no more

DOWN

1. Greek letter
2. Holiday, for one
3. Multitude
4. Strength
5. Receipt word
6. Western Native American
7. What the watchful waiter did?
8. Mines found on Cyprus
9. Dweller in the land of Seir, the country of Edom (Genesis 32:3)
10. Depilatory brand
11. Seaport in Lebanon
16. Recline
20. Repast
21. Fierce wind of the Adriatic
22. Aid's ally
23. What's left
24. Heavenly beings (Fr.)
26. Earnest attempt
27. Blood and guts
28. Utopia
29. "If we be ____ with Christ...we shall also live with him" (Romans 6:8)
31. Girl's nickname
34. Resurrection day
35. "A word fitly spoken is like ____ of gold" (Proverbs 25:11)
37. Supplemental income (abbr.)
38. Greek letters
39. Word in a threat
40. Stir up
41. Long in the tooth
44. Anger
45. Actress Gardner
46. Fish trap
47. Double this for (perhaps) fatal flier

1 2 3 4 5 6 7 8 9 10 11
12 13 14
15 16 17
18 19 20
21 22 23 24
25 26 27 28 29
30 31 32
33 34 35
36 37
38 39 40 41
42 43 44 45 46 47
48 49 50
51 52 53

PUZZLE 50

ACROSS

1. Mentor to Samuel
4. "Sir, we would see ____" (John 12:21)
9. Judicial sentence
12. Benign skin tumor
13. City of Hadad (Genesis 36:35)
14. "Out of whose womb came the ___?" (Job 38:29)
15. Apiece (abbr.)
16. Sign
17. ____ of Melchisedec (Hebrews 7:11)
19. "I was ____ in iniquity" (Psalm 51:5)
21. Ask what might have been
22. French possessive pronoun
23. Said goodnight
27. Without a nom or a nom de plume (abbr.)
29. "Simon Peter...went into the sepulchre, and seeth the ____ clothes" (John 20:6)
30. Bible language (abbr.)
31. ___-oni (Rachel's son)
32. Grace
33. Function
34. Son of Judah (Genesis 38:6)
35. Already sold
36. Played a tuba?
37. "Men of low degree...and men of high degree...are altogether ____ than vanity" (Psalm 62:9)
39. One one-thousandth of an inch
40. Ancient Hebrew liquid measure
41. "Dost thou still ____ thine integrity?" (Job 2:9)
44. "I lay in Sion a chief corner ____" (1 Peter 2:6)
46. "Ye ____ men with burdens grievous" (Luke 11:46)
47. Concerning
48. French possessive pronoun
49. "A man's wisdom maketh his face to ____" (Ecclesiastes 8:1)
51. Parts of a yr.
52. Actor Morita
53. Pursues, as the truth
54. "Go to the ____, thou sluggard" (Proverbs 6:6)

DOWN

1. Jacob gave Esau 200 ____ and 20 rams (Genesis 32:13-14)
2. Mother of Dinah
3. Hoosier state (abbr.)
4. Son of Zebedee, and disciple of Jesus
5. Tied
6. "Be ye angry, and ____ not" (Ephesians 4:26)
7. State of Salt Lake (abbr.)
8. "For the bed is ____ than that a man can stretch himself on it" (Isaiah 28:20)
9. New Jersey college
10. Fast point, in tennis
11. ____ your instructions
16. ____ sesame
18. "The ____ of that house was great" (Luke 6:49)
20. Son of Manasseh, king of Judah (2 Kings 21:18)
23. Ohio, for one
24. "John also was baptizing in ____" (John 3:23)
25. "Woe to them that are at ____ in Zion" (Amos 6:1)
26. Popular female fictional detective
27. Brother of Seth
28. Father of Salathiel (Luke 3:27)

29. Gennesaret, for one
32. "Let your soul delight itself in ____" (Isaiah 55:2)
33. Father of Arah (1 Chronicles 7:39)
35. Willowy
36. "If ye ____ and devour one another, take heed" (Galatians 5:15)
38. Holy ___
39. Overtakers of Babylon
41. Sergeant, for example
42. ____ horse
43. Aerie
44. Brand of automobile oil
45. Orange Pekoe, for example
46. "The highways ____ waste, the wayfaring man ceaseth" (Isaiah 33:8)
50. Pronoun
51. Sturbridge state (abbr.)

ANSWERS

Puzzle 1

W	A	S	T	■	W	A	D	S	■	A	R	E
A	S	E	R	■	A	B	I	A	■	M	E	R
S	P	R	E	A	D	I	N	G	S	■	F	A
■	■	■	A	R	I	D	■	E	T	T	E	S
S	H	A	D	E	■	E	N	■	A	E	R	■
L	A	P	■	L	O	S	E	■	T	R	E	E
O	B	T	A	I	N	■	S	T	E	R	N	S
G	I	F	T	■	C	A	S	H	■	O	C	T
■	T	O	T	T	E	R	■	A	G	R	E	E
M	A	R	A	H	■	R	A	R	E	■	■	■
A	B	■	I	R	R	I	G	A	T	I	O	N
S	L	Y	■	E	A	V	E	■	U	L	A	N
T	E	R	■	E	W	E	S	■	P	E	R	E

Puzzle 2

S	U	P	■	H	O	L	E	S	■	S	O	N
T	R	A	■	E	V	E	N	T	■	T	W	O
E	N	T	E	R	E	D	■	A	M	E	N	D
■	■	I	R	O	N	■	S	T	A	R	■	■
S	H	E	R	D	■	J	O	U	R	N	E	Y
H	E	N	S	■	H	O	O	E	Y	■	R	E
E	A	T	■	C	O	I	N	S	■	E	R	A
M	R	■	V	A	I	N	■	■	A	V	E	R
■	T	H	I	R	S	T	■	S	H	E	D	S
■	■	A	B	E	T	■	B	E	A	N	■	■
T	H	I	E	F	■	G	R	A	Z	I	N	G
O	A	R	■	U	R	I	E	L	■	N	E	E
P	L	Y	■	L	A	N	D	S	■	G	O	T

Puzzle 3

L	I	T	■	E	R	I	C	■	D	R	O	P
E	R	A	■	K	O	O	L	■	A	C	R	E
T	A	B	R	E	T	■	A	R	M	■	G	A
■	■	L	A	D	■	C	I	D	■	M	A	R
O	B	E	Y	■	G	Y	M	■	B	A	N	S
N	E	T	■	S	U	M	■	R	E	D	■	■
E	D	■	T	I	M	B	R	E	L	■	S	A
■	■	E	A	T	■	A	I	L	■	H	A	D
S	O	N	G	■	E	L	M	■	M	A	D	E
O	L	D	■	W	A	S	■	P	A	L	■	■
R	I	■	A	I	R	■	T	I	T	T	L	E
E	V	E	R	■	E	V	E	N	■	E	A	R
S	E	A	T	■	D	I	N	E	■	D	Y	E

Puzzle 4

B	A	R	S	■	G	L	A	S	S	■	D	O
E	■	H	A	I	L	■	D	I	E	■	E	X
E	N	■	P	R	A	Y	■	R	E	A	P	■
N	O	T	■	E	D	E	N	■	D	R	O	P
■	S	O	S	■	■	L	E	D	■	E	R	R
B	E	S	T	■	P	L	E	A	D	■	T	I
E	■	S	E	A	L	■	D	Y	E	D	■	D
A	S	■	P	I	E	T	Y	■	N	A	M	E
S	T	E	■	R	A	W	■	■	S	U	E	■
T	O	L	D	■	T	I	R	E	■	B	A	T
■	D	I	E	T	■	N	E	A	R	■	N	O
A	G	■	F	A	D	■	E	R	A	S	■	R
W	Y	■	Y	I	E	L	D	■	M	A	D	E

Puzzle 5

■	H	A	I	R	S	■	R	A	G	E	S	■
S	U	N	S	E	T	■	E	V	A	D	E	S
P	S	T	■	P	U	R	S	E	■	S	A	P
O	H	■	■	■	P	O	U	R	■	■	M	I
R	A	S	E	■	O	I	L	■	B	A	A	L
T	I	M	B	E	R	■	T	A	L	E	N	T
■	■	E	O	N	■	■	■	R	E	S	■	■
S	T	A	N	D	S	■	R	E	S	O	R	T
V	E	R	Y	■	U	S	E	■	S	P	U	R
E	N	■	■	P	R	I	S	M	■	■	N	E
N	O	R	■	A	E	R	I	E	■	I	N	N
S	N	A	I	L	S	■	D	A	N	C	E	D
■	S	W	E	E	T	■	E	L	D	E	R	■

Puzzle 6

O	W	E	■	W	H	E	A	T	■	T	A	U
W	E	N	■	H	E	A	V	I	N	E	S	S
N	A	T	I	O	N	S	■	■	E	A	S	E
■	R	E	D	■	S	T	R	A	W	■	■	■
F	I	R	E	S	■	■	A	N	■	O	S	A
O	N	■	A	L	A	R	M	S	■	A	W	S
C	E	N	S	E	R	■	A	W	A	K	E	S
U	S	O	■	E	I	T	H	E	R	■	E	N
S	S	W	■	P	E	R	■	R	O	O	T	S
■	■	■	I	S	L	A	M	■	D	A	N	■
A	R	A	M	■	■	D	E	S	I	R	E	S
H	A	P	P	I	N	E	S	S	■	■	S	A
A	N	T	■	N	U	R	S	E	■	E	S	O

Puzzle 7

A	R	E	■	S	E	E	R	S	■	M	A	N
P	A	T	■	T	E	N	E	T	■	E	R	E
T	H	E	L	O	R	D	L	I	V	E	T	H
■	■	R	E	P	■	■	■	R	O	T	■	■
H	A	N	G	S	■	■	A	R	I	S	E	S
A	L	A	S	■	C	I	T	E	D	■	X	I
M	I	L	■	O	I	L	E	D	■	S	I	N
A	V	■	E	N	T	E	R	■	B	A	L	K
N	E	A	T	L	Y	■	■	S	A	V	E	S
■	■	B	U	Y	■	■	■	■	A	I	■	■
P	R	A	I	S	E	T	H	E	L	O	R	D
H	A	S	■	O	D	O	U	R	■	U	T	E
I	N	E	■	N	O	T	E	S	■	R	E	W

Puzzle 8

B	E	E	■	T	O	G	S	■	P	A	R	T
A	S	A	■	A	L	O	E	■	I	L	A	I
Y	E	S	■	N	I	L	E	■	A	I	M	S
■	K	I	N	G	O	F	K	I	N	G	S	■
■	■	E	E	L	S	■	I	R	O	N	■	■
W	A	S	T	E	■	G	N	U	■	■	E	A
A	N	T	S	■	T	A	G	■	D	O	W	N
N	Y	■	■	W	H	Y	■	T	O	W	E	D
■	■	S	T	A	R	■	S	H	O	E	■	■
■	L	O	R	D	O	F	L	O	R	D	S	■
H	I	R	E	■	N	A	U	M	■	H	U	T
A	N	T	E	■	E	Z	R	A	■	I	R	E
M	E	S	S	■	S	E	■	S	■	M	E	N

Puzzle 9

M	A	R	■	C	H	O	P	■	R	A	R	E
E	R	E	■	H	A	R	E	■	E	R	I	E
T	E	D	■	O	R	E	N	■	M	E	D	E
■	■	E	A	S	T	■	N	O	I	S	E	S
T	H	E	M	E	■	P	I	N	T	■	■	■
W	O	M	E	N	■	L	E	E	■	F	E	D
O	M	E	N	■	H	A	S	■	R	A	L	E
S	E	R	■	D	E	N	■	F	A	L	S	E
■	■	■	M	O	A	T	■	E	N	T	E	R
R	E	P	E	N	T	■	R	A	T	E	■	■
E	V	E	R	■	H	O	U	R	■	R	E	D
N	E	A	R	■	E	L	S	E	■	E	R	R
O	N	L	Y	■	N	E	E	D	■	D	A	Y

Puzzle 10

■	N	A	I	L	S	■	B	R	E	E	D	■
L	E	A	V	E	N	■	R	E	N	T	E	D
E	A	R	■	S	A	R	A	I	■	A	L	E
A	R	■	■	T	R	A	I	N	■	■	U	B
V	E	I	L	■	E	N	D	■	M	L	X	I
E	R	R	O	R	S	■	S	L	A	Y	E	R
■	■	O	A	T	■	■	■	A	R	D	■	■
B	A	N	D	E	D	■	L	Y	S	I	A	S
L	E	S	S	■	E	R	A	■	H	A	L	T
E	N	■	■	D	A	I	S	Y	■	■	I	A
S	E	A	■	A	L	P	H	A	■	P	E	N
S	A	D	D	L	E	■	E	R	R	A	N	D
■	S	E	V	E	R	■	S	N	I	T	S	■

Puzzle 11

A	R	E	■	R	I	S	E	S	■	H	A	S
M	A	D	■	U	R	K	E	L	■	A	B	E
E	T	■	A	S	S	Y	R	I	A	■	B	E
N	E	E	D	S	■	■	■	V	I	S	E	D
■	■	P	O	E	T	■	H	E	L	P	■	■
E	L	I	■	T	R	U	E	R	■	I	D	A
T	I	S	■	■	A	S	A	■	■	R	O	W
A	P	T	■	S	M	A	R	T	■	I	C	E
■	■	L	A	M	P	■	D	E	B	T	■	■
T	H	E	R	E	■	■	■	R	E	S	I	N
R	E	■	T	A	R	R	I	E	D	■	S	O
O	R	E	■	R	A	I	L	S	■	A	L	A
W	E	N	■	S	T	A	L	E	■	N	E	H

Puzzle 12

D	A	W	N	■	A	E	R	■	R	O	P	E
A	R	I	A	■	B	E	E	■	E	D	E	N
N	E	S	T	■	I	L	L	■	C	O	R	E
■	S	H	I	E	D	■	A	L	A	R	M	■
■	■	■	O	N	E	■	T	E	N	■	■	■
A	T	O	N	E	S	■	E	A	T	I	N	G
W	O	N	■	■	■	■	■	■	■	N	E	O
L	O	O	S	E	D	■	B	A	S	K	E	T
■	■	■	T	O	E	■	U	S	E	■	■	■
■	M	O	R	N	S	■	R	A	L	E	D	■
M	O	P	E	■	I	N	N	■	L	A	I	R
A	L	E	E	■	R	O	E	■	E	S	A	U
P	E	N	T	■	E	N	D	■	R	E	L	S

Puzzle 13

S	A	M	■	G	E	T	S	■	R	I	D	E
A	G	E	■	L	A	I	C	■	E	N	O	N
F	A	T	H	E	R	■	A	B	A	S	E	D
E	R	R	E	D	■	■	R	A	C	E	■	■
■	■	I	T	E	M	S	■	S	H	R	E	W
S	U	C	H	■	E	T	A	T	■	T	E	E
T	N	■	■	B	L	A	M	E	■	■	R	N
A	D	E	■	E	T	R	E	■	B	O	■	S
R	O	U	S	E	■	E	N	D	O	R	■	■
■	■	N	E	R	I	■	■	E	R	A	S	E
S	P	I	R	I	T	■	D	A	N	C	E	S
E	N	C	E	■	C	A	I	N	■	L	E	A
T	■	E	D	■	H	I	S	S	■	E	M	U

Puzzle 14

E	R	S	■	T	A	S	K	S	■	M	A	D
S	A	P	■	A	L	E	P	H	■	A	D	O
S	W	A	L	L	O	W	■	E	A	T	E	N
■	■	R	I	O	T	■	S	A	L	T	■	■
C	A	R	O	N	■	S	E	R	P	E	N	T
A	N	O	N	■	H	A	R	E	S	■	O	R
L	O	W	■	C	O	V	E	R	■	A	B	E
E	D	■	S	A	V	E	■	■	A	B	L	E
B	E	E	T	L	E	S	■	C	R	I	E	S
■	■	N	E	L	L	■	R	O	A	D	■	■
T	H	E	M	E	■	N	U	M	B	E	R	S
I	A	M	■	S	H	E	E	P	■	T	I	E
S	T	Y	■	T	O	A	D	S	■	H	O	T

Puzzle 15

■	■	■	■	■	■	■	A	T	A	D	■	■
■	■	■	R	T	E	■	S	A	L	E	S	■
■	■	S	O	U	R	■	S	U	P	P	E	D
■	S	U	P	R	E	M	E	■	■	O	A	R
■	O	M	E	N	■	E	N	■	I	S	L	E
■	■	■	■	■	R	A	T	■	T	E	E	D
■	A	L	L	■	E	S	E	■	O	D	D	■
P	L	E	A	■	C	U	D	■	■	■	■	■
A	M	O	S	■	O	R	■	H	O	P	E	■
S	O	P	■	■	R	E	C	O	V	E	R	■
S	N	A	R	E	D	■	A	M	E	N	■	■
■	D	R	O	V	E	■	B	E	N	■	■	■
■	■	D	E	E	D	■	■	■	■	■	■	■

Puzzle 16

R	O	B	■	■	H	A	L	F	■	O	H	M
E	N	O	S	■	O	L	E	O	■	B	O	A
A	C	R	E	■	E	T	E	R	N	I	T	Y
L	E	N	T	■	■	■	■	M	I	■	■	■
■	■	A	S	I	D	E	■	S	L	A	V	E
L	E	G	■	C	E	L	L	■	■	G	E	L
A	S	A	■	E	N	D	E	D	■	R	I	M
H	A	I	■	■	T	E	A	R	■	E	L	S
R	U	N	N	Y	■	R	H	Y	M	E	■	■
■	■	■	O	E	D	■	■	■	O	M	E	R
S	T	E	W	A	R	D	S	■	S	E	M	I
E	E	R	■	R	A	I	L	■	S	N	I	P
E	Y	E	■	S	W	A	Y	■	■	T	R	E

Puzzle 17

■	■	C	A	V	E	■	F	L	O	W	■	■
■	B	A	T	O	N	■	L	I	G	H	T	■
S	I	N	E	W	■	S	U	P	■	Y	E	T
A	S	E	■	■	N	U	T	S	■	■	N	O
L	O	■	■	C	A	S	E	■	S	T	O	P
E	N	D	■	A	M	A	■	L	I	O	N	S
■	■	R	A	G	E	■	N	O	N	E	■	■
S	H	A	R	E	■	D	E	N	■	S	E	W
H	U	G	E	■	P	A	T	E	■	■	M	E
O	N	■	■	S	I	R	S	■	S	T	I	R
E	T	E	■	H	E	N	■	S	H	A	M	E
■	S	A	D	O	C	■	H	A	U	L	S	■
■	■	R	O	D	E	■	T	Y	R	E	■	■

Puzzle 18

G	I	L	D	■	H	E	L	P	■	S	T	E
A	R	E	A	■	P	L	E	A	■	P	E	A
P	E	A	R	L	■	M	E	R	■	L	A	T
■	■	■	K	I	D	■	S	T	A	I	R	S
S	L	E	E	P	E	R	■	N	E	T	■	■
T	O	R	N	■	T	A	M	E	R	■	H	O
U	S	E	■	S	E	N	O	R	■	M	A	N
B	E	■	B	A	R	G	E	■	L	A	T	E
■	■	C	A	N	■	E	S	C	A	P	E	S
B	R	A	N	D	S	■	■	A	W	■	■	■
E	A	R	■	A	L	L	■	L	Y	D	I	A
A	R	E	■	L	A	I	R	■	E	O	N	S
R	E	D	■	S	P	I	N	■	R	E	N	E

Puzzle 19

A	N	G	E	■	A	D	A	M	■	A	R	M
R	O	L	L	■	P	A	R	A	■	C	O	O
T	R	O	D	■	E	M	I	R	■	R	E	O
■	■	R	E	A	D	S	■	C	H	E	S	T
T	H	I	R	D	■	■	S	H	E	■	■	■
R	I	O	■	S	E	A	T	■	A	M	O	S
E	L	U	L	■	D	Y	E	■	L	I	V	E
E	L	S	E	■	G	E	M	S	■	N	E	E
■	■	■	A	T	E	■	■	T	H	I	N	K
S	H	A	P	E	■	F	L	E	E	S	■	■
O	E	R	■	A	R	I	A	■	A	T	A	D
R	A	M	■	C	O	S	T	■	R	E	B	A
T	R	Y	■	H	O	T	E	■	T	R	I	G

Puzzle 20

B	E	L	■	S	H	E	B	A	■	D	A	Y
A	P	E	■	P	A	N	E	L	■	R	I	E
S	I	N	N	E	R	S	■	M	A	I	D	S
■	■	T	I	N	E	■	L	O	V	E	■	■
S	P	I	L	T	■	V	E	N	I	S	O	N
M	U	L	E	■	B	I	N	D	S	■	M	A
E	L	S	■	L	A	N	D	S	■	H	E	M
A	S	■	S	O	R	E	S	■	S	A	G	E
R	E	D	U	C	E	S	■	P	A	P	A	S
■	■	O	N	U	S	■	H	E	L	P	■	■
L	E	E	K	S	■	M	E	N	T	I	O	N
A	N	S	■	T	R	A	I	N	■	E	R	E
G	E	T	■	S	O	R	R	Y	■	R	E	D

Puzzle 21

P	S	A	L	M	S	■	■	T	H	A	R	A
R	E	S	I	D	E	S	■	R	A	G	E	S
A	L	T	■	S	A	T	■	I	R	O	N	S
M	A	I	L	■	L	O	V	E	D	■	D	E
S	H	R	E	W	■	R	I	D	■	T	E	N
■	■	■	N	A	M	E	S	■	D	I	R	T
■	P	E	D	R	O	■	I	D	O	L	S	■
E	R	E	S	■	U	N	T	I	E	■	■	■
S	E	L	■	P	R	E	■	A	S	H	E	R
H	P	■	M	A	N	S	E	■	T	A	L	E
K	A	M	E	L	■	T	A	R	■	I	D	E
O	R	A	T	E	■	S	T	I	R	R	E	D
L	E	P	E	R	■	■	S	A	T	Y	R	S

Puzzle 22

L	A	M	B	■	A	B	E	L	■	T	E	A
A	R	E	A	■	R	A	V	E	■	R	A	W
W	E	A	K	■	T	R	E	A	S	U	R	E
■	■	S	E	T	S	■	■	S	P	E	N	D
C	R	U	D	E	■	B	E	T	A	■	■	■
A	I	R	■	A	T	A	D	■	S	P	A	T
I	C	E	■	R	A	R	E	R	■	R	U	E
N	E	S	T	■	L	A	N	A	■	E	N	D
■	■	■	I	N	C	■	■	T	E	S	T	S
O	P	H	N	I	■	■	B	E	D	S	■	■
P	L	E	A	S	U	R	E	■	G	U	L	F
E	E	R	■	A	S	I	A	■	E	R	I	E
N	A	B	■	N	E	A	R	■	D	E	E	D

Puzzle 23

1 T	2 S	3 P	■	4 A	5 L	6 O	7 N	8 E	■	9 S	10 P	11 A
12 O	I	L	13 S	■	14 O	P	E	N	■	15 H	A	S
16 S	T	O	L	17 E	■	18 T	A	S	19 T	E	T	H
■	■	20 W	A	R	■	■	21 T	I	E	R	S	■
22 T	23 R	I	V	I	24 A	25 L	■	26 G	A	D	■	■
27 R	E	N	E	■	28 L	I	29 O	N	S	■	30 A	31 T
32 E	N	G	■	33 A	M	A	S	S	■	34 O	D	E
35 E	T	■	36 C	H	A	R	T	■	37 A	N	O	N
■	■	38 A	H	A	■	39 S	E	40 A	L	E	S	T
■	41 G	R	A	Z	42 E	■	43 O	M	I	T	■	■
44 M	O	O	R	I	N	45 G	■	46 T	A	H	47 O	48 E
49 E	R	S	■	50 A	V	E	51 R	■	52 S	A	R	I
53 N	E	E	■	54 H	Y	E	N	A	■	55 T	A	N

Puzzle 24

1 J	2 A	3 Y	■	4 A	5 S	6 P	■	7 H	8 E	9 M	■	■
10 O	W	E	■	11 N	E	T	■	12 E	N	O	13 S	■
14 Y	E	L	15 L	O	W	■	16 D	I	D	■	17 H	18 A
■	■	19 P	I	N	■	20 M	A	R	■	21 S	O	S
22 L	23 A	S	T	■	24 M	A	N	■	25 B	A	T	H
26 O	G	■	■	27 B	E	D	■	28 P	E	N	■	■
29 G	O	30 L	31 D	E	N	■	32 D	I	G	G	33 E	34 D
■	■	35 E	Y	E	■	36 H	O	T	■	■	37 A	R
38 D	39 I	N	E	■	40 W	A	G	■	41 D	42 U	T	Y
43 A	R	T	■	44 T	A	P	■	45 S	I	P	■	■
46 M	A	■	47 F	I	R	■	48 T	E	M	P	49 E	50 R
■	51 M	52 E	A	N	■	53 B	E	N	■	54 E	L	F
■	■	55 D	R	Y	■	56 E	N	D	■	57 R	I	D

Puzzle 25

1 F	2 I	3 R	■	4 L	5 A	6 M	7 P	■	8 L	9 E	10 S	11 S
12 A	C	E	■	13 I	D	O	L	■	14 I	R	O	N
15 R	E	M	16 O	V	E	■	17 A	18 R	E	■	19 L	O
■	■	20 A	W	E	■	21 A	N	T	■	22 D	E	W
23 R	24 A	I	L	■	25 A	P	T	■	26 E	A	S	Y
27 U	R	N	■	28 S	I	P	■	29 C	A	Y	■	■
30 N	M	■	31 T	E	L	L	32 E	S	T	■	33 H	34 O
■	■	35 L	O	W	■	36 I	R	A	■	37 F	E	W
38 S	39 H	O	E	■	40 S	E	E	■	41 L	A	M	E
42 H	I	T	■	43 S	A	D	■	44 W	E	T	■	■
45 A	R	■	46 A	R	K	■	47 M	I	G	H	48 T	49 Y
50 D	E	51 A	R	■	52 E	53 D	E	N	■	54 E	W	E
55 E	D	I	T	■	56 S	O	N	G	■	57 R	O	T

Puzzle 26

1 M	2 I	3 S	4 S	■	5 B	6 E	7 A	8 R	■	9 E	10 R	11 E
12 A	R	C	H	■	13 E	L	S	E	■	14 R	O	W
15 A	S	H	E	16 R	■	■	17 P	L	18 E	A	S	E
■	■	19 O	R	E	20 O	■	■	21 E	A	S	E	S
22 P	23 R	O	D	U	C	24 T	■	25 A	R	E	■	■
26 O	I	L	■	■	27 C	R	28 O	S	S	■	29 L	30 B
31 L	O	■	■	32 G	U	I	L	E	■	■	33 A	I
34 E	T	■	35 C	A	R	E	D	■	■	36 A	T	E
■	■	37 H	U	R	■	38 D	E	39 L	40 I	V	E	R
41 S	42 T	O	R	M	■	■	43 R	I	S	E	■	■
44 A	S	L	E	E	45 P	■	■	46 T	A	R	47 A	48 H
49 G	A	D	■	50 N	A	51 M	52 E	■	53 A	S	I	A
54 E	R	S	■	55 T	W	I	N	■	56 C	E	L	T

Puzzle 27

■	■	1 O	2 W	3 L	4 S	■	5 S	6 L	7 A	8 P	■	■
■	9 T	R	I	A	L	■	10 T	A	M	E	11 D	■
12 G	R	A	N	D	E	■	13 A	D	O	R	A	14 M
15 O	A	T	■	16 D	E	17 N	Y	■	18 S	I	N	E
19 A	L	O	20 E	■	21 P	A	I	22 R	■	23 S	C	I
24 L	A	R	G	25 E	■	26 G	N	A	27 S	H	E	R
■	■	■	28 G	A	29 P	■	30 G	I	N	■	■	■
31 B	32 L	33 E	S	S	E	34 S	■	35 N	O	36 B	37 L	38 E
39 L	U	R	■	40 T	O	U	41 R	■	42 W	E	E	D
43 E	T	R	44 E	■	45 P	R	A	46 Y	■	47 E	V	E
48 W	E	A	S	49 E	L	■	50 H	E	51 A	V	E	N
■	52 S	N	A	K	E	■	53 A	L	T	E	R	■
■	■	54 D	U	E	S	■	55 B	L	T	S	■	■

Puzzle 28

1 S	2 I	3 R	4 S	■	5 A	6 C	7 R	8 E	■	9 O	10 W	11 L
12 P	O	E	T	■	13 R	O	A	D	■	14 P	O	E
15 A	N	N	A	■	16 E	M	S	■	17 N	E	E	D
■	■	18 E	G	19 G	■	20 B	E	21 G	I	N	■	■
■	22 S	W	E	A	23 R	■	24 D	O	T	■	25 A	26 S
27 C	L	I	■	28 D	A	29 M	■	30 D	R	31 O	V	E
32 L	I	N	33 E	■	34 M	A	35 D	■	36 E	V	E	R
37 A	N	G	R	38 Y	■	39 R	U	40 E	■	41 E	R	E
42 P	G	■	43 R	E	44 D	■	45 E	N	46 T	R	Y	■
■	■	47 B	O	A	R	48 D	■	49 S	E	C	■	■
50 S	51 E	E	R	■	52 E	A	53 T	■	54 R	O	55 B	56 E
57 A	W	L	■	58 B	A	R	E	■	59 A	M	O	S
60 Y	E	T	■	61 E	D	E	N	■	62 H	E	A	T

Puzzle 29

1 T	2 A	3 M	4 A	■	5 R	6 O	7 M	8 E	■	9 W	10 A	11 R
12 E	L	A	M	■	13 A	N	E	M	■	14 E	L	I
15 N	A	■	16 E	17 D	G	E	■	■	18 R	E	A	P
■	■	19 T	R	U	E	■	20 S	21 T	Y	■	22 B	E
23 P	24 R	I	C	E	■	25 T	H	I	E	26 F	■	■
27 L	A	T	E	■	28 S	H	A	M	■	29 O	30 D	31 D
32 A	S	H	■	33 S	P	A	R	E	■	34 R	O	E
35 N	E	E	■	36 T	I	N	E	■	37 A	G	U	E
■	■	38 S	39 T	I	C	K	■	40 S	W	O	R	D
41 S	42 H	■	43 A	R	E	■	44 M	E	A	T	■	■
45 T	O	46 W	N	■	■	47 L	E	A	K	■	48 E	49 R
50 O	A	R	■	51 A	52 R	I	A	■	53 E	54 A	S	E
55 P	R	Y	■	56 M	E	E	T	■	57 N	E	E	D

Puzzle 30

1 J	2 A	3 W	■	4 P	5 A	6 R	7 E	■	8 A	9 I	10 L	11 S
12 A	B	E	■	13 E	B	O	N	■	14 S	N	E	E
15 W	E	A	16 K	E	N	E	D	■	17 S	C	A	R
18 S	T	R	I	P	E	■	■	19 O	I	L	■	■
■	■	■	20 T	E	R	■	21 A	R	R	O	22 W	23 S
24 D	25 I	26 N	E	D	■	27 A	R	E	■	28 S	E	E
29 A	R	E	S	■	30 O	L	D	■	31 C	E	R	T
32 T	O	I	■	33 A	W	L	■	34 R	I	D	E	S
35 E	N	G	36 A	G	E	■	37 B	E	T	■	■	■
■	■	38 H	I	E	■	■	39 A	M	E	40 R	41 C	42 E
43 R	44 I	B	S	■	45 F	46 O	R	E	S	H	I	P
47 I	D	O	L	■	48 O	D	E	D	■	49 E	T	E
50 D	A	R	E	■	51 E	D	D	Y	■	52 A	Y	E

Puzzle 31

1 B	2 A	3 R	■	4 A	5 S	6 H	7 E	8 R	■	9 A	10 S	11 A
12 A	R	T	■	13 S	T	A	T	E	■	14 D	E	L
15 B	E	■	16 F	L	E	S	H	L	17 Y	■	18 E	A
19 E	A	20 G	L	E	■	■	■	21 I	R	22 O	N	S
■	■	23 E	Y	E	24 S	■	25 N	E	S	T	■	■
26 D	27 A	N	■	28 P	29 L	E	A	D	■	30 H	31 E	32 M
33 A	R	E	■	■	34 A	R	M	■	■	35 N	O	E
36 M	A	R	■	37 T	I	R	E	38 S	■	39 I	N	N
■	■	40 A	41 N	O	N	■	42 S	I	43 D	E	■	■
44 B	45 A	L	A	K	■	■	■	46 R	O	L	47 L	48 S
49 A	M	■	50 P	51 E	52 O	53 P	L	E	S	■	54 A	A
55 T	O	56 W	■	57 N	I	S	A	N	■	58 P	I	N
59 S	K	Y	■	60 S	L	I	P	S	■	61 A	R	K

Puzzle 32

1 S	2 A	3 L	4 E	■	5 C	6 A	7 R	8 E	■	9 T	10 O	11 W
12 A	M	O	S	■	13 A	M	E	N	■	14 E	W	E
15 P	I	■	16 T	17 E	N	T	■	■	18 B	E	E	S
■	■	19 P	A	R	E	■	20 P	21 S	I	■	22 S	T
23 C	24 R	E	T	E	■	25 S	A	I	T	26 H	■	■
27 R	A	R	E	■	28 T	H	I	N	■	29 A	30 H	31 A
32 I	C	I	■	33 T	H	A	N	K	■	34 P	A	N
35 B	E	L	■	36 O	I	L	S	■	37 S	P	I	T
■	■	38 S	39 H	O	R	T	■	40 S	E	E	R	S
41 O	42 H	■	43 O	L	D	■	44 B	E	E	N	■	■
45 M	E	46 A	T	■	■	47 M	E	E	T	■	48 A	49 I
50 E	R	R	■	51 O	52 P	E	N	■	53 H	54 E	I	R
55 R	O	E	■	56 W	O	N	T	■	57 E	A	R	S

Puzzle 33

1 S	2 T	3 A	4 R	■	5 T	6 R	7 Y	■	8 S	9 E	10 M	11 I
12 E	A	S	E	■	13 H	O	E	■	14 L	A	I	R
15 A	R	I	A	■	16 E	A	T	■	17 A	C	R	E
18 S	E	A	S	19 O	N	S	■	20 A	C	H	E	■
■	■	■	21 O	W	■	22 T	23 A	S	K	■	■	■
24 S	25 T	26 O	N	E	■	■	27 H	A	■	28 D	29 E	30 W
31 O	W	N	S	■	■	■	■	■	32 S	U	R	E
33 D	O	E	■	34 B	35 E	■	■	36 S	T	E	A	D
■	■	■	37 D	E	N	38 S	■	39 U	R	■	■	■
■	40 L	41 E	O	N	■	42 T	43 R	E	A	44 D	45 E	46 D
47 W	A	G	E	■	48 A	R	E	■	49 N	O	N	O
50 E	T	A	S	■	51 N	I	L	■	52 G	O	O	N
53 B	E	L	T	■	54 S	P	Y	■	55 E	R	N	E

Puzzle 34

1 M	2 A	3 R	4 A	■	5 F	6 O	7 A	8 M	■	9 D	10 O	11 A
12 O	R	E	B	■	13 I	D	L	E	■	14 R	U	B
15 W	A	S	H	■	16 L	O	A	D	■	17 E	S	E
■	■	18 T	O	19 W	E	R	■	20 E	21 M	I	T	S
22 S	23 H	O	R	E	■	■	24 U	S	A	■	■	■
25 A	I	R	■	26 B	27 E	28 E	N	■	29 H	30 A	31 L	32 F
33 I	D	E	34 A	■	35 L	A	D	■	36 I	D	O	L
37 L	E	S	S	■	38 S	T	O	39 P	■	40 O	N	E
■	■	■	41 E	42 W	E	■	■	43 R	44 O	P	E	D
45 S	46 H	47 A	R	E	■	48 W	49 H	E	A	T	■	■
50 T	A	X	■	51 A	52 S	I	A	■	53 T	I	54 R	55 E
56 A	R	E	■	57 R	E	S	T	■	58 H	O	U	R
59 Y	E	S	■	60 S	A	T	E	■	61 S	N	E	E

Puzzle 35

1 E	2 W	3 E	4 S	■	5 I	6 L	7 L	■	8 C	9 H	10 E	11 W
12 H	I	N	T	■	13 N	O	A	■	14 O	A	T	H
15 U	N	D	O	■	16 H	U	N	■	17 A	R	E	A
18 D	E	S	I	19 R	E	■	20 C	21 H	R	I	S	T
■	■	■	22 C	A	R	■	23 E	S	S	■	■	■
24 W	25 O	26 R	S	H	I	27 P	■	28 T	E	29 N	30 T	31 S
32 E	V	E	■	■	33 T	I	34 P	■	■	35 A	I	U
36 T	A	U	37 N	38 T	■	39 T	R	40 A	41 M	P	L	E
■	■	■	42 E	A	43 R	■	44 A	R	E	■	■	■
45 S	46 T	47 A	T	U	E	■	48 I	M	A	49 G	50 E	51 S
52 W	I	S	H	■	53 A	54 S	S	■	55 D	I	V	E
56 A	L	E	E	■	57 L	I	E	■	58 O	V	E	N
59 N	E	A	R	■	60 M	R	S	■	61 W	E	N	T

Puzzle 36

1 A	2 S	3 P	■	4 K	5 I	6 N	7 G	■	8 H	9 O	10 N	11 E
12 P	U	R	■	13 E	S	A	U	■	14 O	S	E	E
15 T	E	E	■	16 D	A	Y	S	■	17 W	H	E	N
■	■	18 S	19 T	A	R	■	■	20 D	E	E	D	■
21 S	22 P	E	A	R	■	23 R	24 H	O	■	A	■	■
25 P	A	N	T	■	26 B	E	A	S	T	■	27 C	28 A
29 A	R	T	■	30 H	E	A	R	T	■	31 S	O	N
32 N	T	■	33 H	E	N	C	E	■	34 W	I	L	T
■	■	35 F	O	R	T	H	■	36 H	A	L	T	S
■	37 T	R	U	E	■	■	38 F	I	R	E	■	■
39 H	I	E	S	■	40 T	41 E	A	R	■	42 N	43 N	44 E
45 A	L	E	E	■	46 R	A	M	A	■	47 C	O	E
48 M	E	S	S	■	49 I	T	E	M	■	50 E	R	E

Puzzle 37

1 M	2 T	3 S	■	4 B	5 A	6 L	7 M	■	8 A	9 H	10 A	11 B
12 I	R	A	■	13 E	R	I	E	■	14 B	A	D	E
15 S	E	T	16 S	■	17 A	S	S	■	18 I	R	O	N
19 T	E	E	T	20 H	■	21 A	S	22 I	D	E	■	■
■	■	■	23 R	E	24 S	■	25 E	N	E	■	26 D	27 O
28 A	29 N	30 O	I	N	T	31 I	N	G	■	32 T	I	N
33 R	E	A	P	■	34 E	R	G	■	35 S	O	R	E
36 M	A	R	■	37 W	A	T	E	38 R	P	O	T	S
39 S	R	■	40 G	O	D	■	41 R	O	E	■	■	■
■	■	42 T	H	E	F	43 T	■	44 D	A	45 N	46 C	47 E
48 A	49 H	I	O	■	50 A	R	51 E	■	52 R	E	A	D
53 H	U	M	S	■	54 S	U	R	55 E	■	56 R	I	E
57 A	B	E	T	■	58 T	E	A	R	■	59 I	N	N

Puzzle 38

1 W	2 A	3 R	4 S	■	5 K	6 E	7 E	8 P	■	9 C	10 A	11 B
12 E	S	E	K	■	13 A	L	A	S	■	14 H	U	E
15 B	A	S	I	16 N	S	■	17 T	A	18 L	E	N	T
■	■	19 U	R	I	M	■	■	20 L	I	E	T	H
21 H	22 A	L	T	S	■	23 D	24 O	M	E	S	■	■
25 A	C	T	■	26 A	27 N	O	N	■	28 S	E	29 L	30 L
31 I	N	■	■	32 N	A	V	E	33 S	■	■	34 I	E
35 L	E	36 S	37 S	■	38 P	E	S	T	■	39 M	E	N
■	■	40 P	O	41 W	E	R	■	42 A	43 M	E	N	D
44 S	45 H	O	N	E	■	■	46 A	L	A	N	■	■
47 L	O	O	S	E	48 D	■	49 S	E	N	S	50 E	51 S
52 I	N	N	■	53 P	I	54 C	K	■	55 N	E	S	T
56 T	E	S	■	57 S	E	A	S	■	58 A	S	P	S

Puzzle 39

1 S	2 C	3 A	4 L	5 P	6 S	■	■	7 S	8 A	9 V	10 E	11 D
12 H	A	S	T	I	L	13 Y	■	14 E	X	I	L	E
15 A	M	I	■	16 T	E	E	■	17 V	I	N	E	S
18 N	E	E	19 T	■	20 W	A	21 G	E	S	■	22 M	I
23 A	L	L	O	24 T	■	25 R	U	N	■	26 M	E	R
■	■	■	27 L	O	28 O	S	E	■	29 M	A	N	E
■	30 P	31 I	L	O	T	■	32 S	33 H	O	R	T	■
34 M	I	L	S	■	35 H	36 A	T	E	S	■	■	■
37 A	T	L	■	38 G	E	L	■	39 M	E	40 T	41 E	42 D
43 D	C	■	44 D	A	R	T	45 S	■	46 S	A	V	E
47 E	H	■	48 O	R	■	49 E	E	50 E	■	51 B	E	E
52 S	53 E	I	N	E	■	54 R	E	S	55 P	O	N	D
56 T	R	E	E	S	■	■	57 S	P	O	R	T	S

Puzzle 40

■	■	1 H	2 A	3 L	4 E	■	5 L	6 E	7 A	8 P	■	■
■	9 S	E	V	E	N	■	10 E	A	G	L	11 E	■
12 T	H	R	E	A	T	■	13 T	R	U	E	S	14 T
15 R	A	M	■	16 K	E	17 P	T	■	18 R	A	T	E
19 A	M	O	20 S	■	21 R	E	E	22 L	■	23 S	E	E
24 P	E	N	N	25 S	■	26 P	R	E	27 F	E	R	S
■	■	■	28 O	P	29 P	■	30 S	A	L	■	■	■
31 F	32 R	33 O	W	A	R	34 D	■	35 F	A	36 D	37 E	38 S
39 O	I	L	■	40 S	A	U	41 L	■	42 T	I	D	E
43 E	V	I	44 L	■	45 Y	E	A	46 R	■	47 A	G	E
48 S	E	V	E	49 R	E	■	50 M	I	51 N	D	E	D
■	52 S	E	V	E	R	■	53 B	O	N	E	S	■
■	■	54 S	I	T	S	■	55 S	T	E	M	■	■

Puzzle 41

M	A	P	■	S	W	A	M	■	S	M	E	E
A	B	I	■	T	A	R	E	■	H	E	A	R
R	E	S	T	O	R	E	D	■	E	A	R	N
S	T	A	I	N	■	S	E	A	T	S	■	■
■	■	■	T	E	A	■	■	S	H	U	N	S
A	R	C	H	■	S	I	G	H	■	R	A	E
P	U	R	E	■	I	L	O	■	R	E	V	E
E	T	E	■	H	A	L	L	■	E	D	E	N
S	H	A	D	E	■	■	D	I	A	■	■	■
■	■	T	E	N	T	H	■	S	L	O	P	E
E	R	I	E	■	R	E	M	E	M	B	E	R
L	O	O	P	■	O	R	A	■	■	E	P	I
M	E	N	S	■	W	A	R	T	■	D	E	E

Puzzle 42

I	R	E	■	S	H	I	P	■	I	D	O	L
T	E	L	■	C	A	L	M	■	M	I	R	E
E	L	I	■	A	L	L	■	S	P	E	E	D
■	■	H	A	T	E	■	S	R	A	■	■	■
T	R	U	S	T	■	G	L	O	R	I	F	Y
I	E	■	A	E	R	I	E	■	T	A	R	E
R	A	E	■	R	I	V	E	R	■	M	A	A
A	C	R	E	■	P	E	T	E	R	■	M	R
S	H	R	I	N	E	S	■	S	E	V	E	N
■	■	■	T	E	N	■	A	T	M	■	■	■
W	I	G	H	T	■	P	L	O	■	F	E	W
E	R	I	E	■	R	E	A	R	■	E	R	E
B	I	E	R	■	R	A	S	E	■	D	A	N

Puzzle 43

■	■	A	X	L	E	■	O	A	T	S	■	■
■	A	B	I	E	L	■	T	R	A	I	N	■
A	R	R	I	V	E	■	H	E	R	M	O	N
A	D	O	■	■	C	A	N	■	■	E	T	A
R	E	A	■	A	T	R	I	A	■	O	E	R
E	N	D	O	W	■	D	E	M	A	N	D	S
■	■	■	H	A	Y	■	L	E	D	■	■	■
S	T	R	O	K	E	S	■	N	O	T	C	H
E	S	E	■	E	A	S	E	D	■	E	H	I
R	A	M	■	■	R	E	S	■	■	M	E	N
A	R	I	S	E	N	■	S	O	P	P	E	D
■	S	T	O	R	E	■	E	N	T	E	R	■
■	■	S	U	E	D	■	N	E	A	R	■	■

Puzzle 44

B	A	D	■	B	R	I	D	E	■	B	A	R
E	P	I	■	R	E	M	I	T	■	I	C	E
D	E	F	I	E	D	■	M	E	N	D	E	D
■	■	F	R	E	D	S	■	R	O	D	■	■
T	R	E	A	D	■	T	E	N	D	E	T	H
H	U	R	T	■	R	I	T	A	■	N	O	E
U	L	■	E	M	E	R	A	L	D	■	W	A
M	E	T	■	E	A	R	S	■	R	A	I	L
B	R	A	I	L	L	E	■	P	O	S	T	S
■	■	S	A	T	■	D	R	A	W	S	■	■
N	U	T	M	E	G	■	O	R	N	E	R	Y
O	R	E	■	T	E	M	P	T	■	N	Y	E
B	E	D	■	H	O	L	E	S	■	T	E	A

Puzzle 45

R	A	M	■	B	E	N	■	S	O	N	■	■
A	D	O	■	E	N	E	■	P	A	U	L	■
W	A	S	T	E	D	■	H	U	R	■	A	H
■	■	E	O	N	■	H	E	N	■	S	T	E
W	A	S	P	■	L	O	W	■	S	T	E	M
A	S	■	■	S	I	T	■	P	E	A	■	■
S	P	R	E	A	D	■	N	E	A	R	L	Y
■	■	O	A	T	■	D	O	N	■	■	I	E
C	O	L	T	■	F	A	T	■	P	L	E	A
A	W	L	■	L	A	Y	■	F	O	E	■	■
B	E	■	A	I	R	■	P	L	E	A	S	E
■	D	E	C	K	■	V	I	A	■	R	U	N
■	■	A	T	E	■	A	N	T	■	N	E	E

Puzzle 46

A	M	A	N	A	■	■	■	K	I	T	E	S
R	E	F	I	N	E	■	S	N	E	E	Z	E
M	E	T	■	N	L	■	H	I	■	E	R	A
S	T	■	D	U	S	T	O	F	F	■	A	L
■	■	B	E	L	I	E	V	E	R	S	■	■
B	A	R	S	■	E	N	E	■	O	H	I	O
E	X	I	T	■	■	■	■	■	W	I	D	E
D	E	E	R	■	G	T	O	■	A	P	E	R
■	■	F	O	L	L	O	W	E	R	S	■	■
E	R	■	Y	E	A	R	N	E	D	■	G	P
R	E	O	■	A	N	■	E	R	■	B	I	O
R	E	W	A	R	D	■	R	I	V	E	R	S
S	K	E	I	N	■	■	■	E	A	G	L	E

Puzzle 47

O	E	R	■	R	A	N	G	E	■	P	A	N
A	R	E	■	I	D	O	L	S	■	R	I	A
F	R	I	E	N	D	■	E	A	S	I	L	Y
■	■	G	A	G	■	T	A	U	P	E	■	■
L	E	N	T	■	D	I	M	■	I	S	L	E
E	N	S	■	S	I	N	■	E	N	T	E	R
A	D	■	S	I	N	G	E	R	S	■	P	G
V	O	W	E	D	■	L	A	■	■	R	E	■
E	W	E	R	■	V	E	T	■	H	E	R	D
■	■	A	V	O	I	D	■	S	A	D	■	■
B	A	K	E	R	S	■	S	I	L	E	N	T
O	W	E	■	E	I	G	H	T	■	E	O	N
W	E	N	■	■	T	O	Y	S	■	M	E	T

Puzzle 48

S	E	A	S	■	A	B	D	A	■	A	R	E
I	T	C	H	■	N	A	I	L	■	M	E	R
R	A	C	E	■	T	R	A	P	■	E	A	R
■	■	E	E	R	I	E	■	H	A	N	D	S
H	A	P	P	Y	■	■	T	A	B	■	■	■
E	S	T	■	E	A	S	E	■	B	A	N	D
L	I	E	S	■	G	I	N	■	A	L	O	E
L	A	D	E	■	U	N	D	O	■	T	O	E
■	■	■	E	R	E	■	■	A	M	E	N	D
C	H	I	D	E	■	E	R	R	O	R	■	■
H	I	D	■	S	I	D	E	■	L	E	V	I
O	R	E	■	T	R	E	E	■	E	T	A	L
P	E	A	■	S	E	N	D	■	S	H	U	L

Puzzle 49

T	I	M	E	■	P	U	R	■	C	E	N	T
A	N	O	N	■	A	T	E	■	O	S	A	Y
U	N	B	E	L	I	E	F	■	P	A	I	R
■	■	■	R	I	D	■	I	M	P	U	R	E
B	A	R	G	E	■	A	L	E	E	■	■	■
O	B	E	Y	■	E	N	L	A	R	G	E	D
R	E	S	■	A	N	G	E	L	■	O	D	E
A	T	T	E	N	D	E	D	■	A	R	E	A
■	■	■	A	D	E	S	■	S	P	E	N	D
P	E	R	S	I	A	■	A	S	P	■	■	■
S	L	I	T	■	V	I	G	I	L	A	N	T
I	S	L	E	■	O	R	E	■	E	V	E	S
S	E	E	R	■	R	E	D	■	S	A	T	E

Puzzle 50

E	L	I	■	J	E	S	U	S	■	R	A	P
W	E	N	■	A	V	I	T	H	■	I	C	E
E	A	■	O	M	E	N	■	O	R	D	E	R
S	H	A	P	E	N	■	■	R	U	E	■	■
■	■	M	E	S	■	R	E	T	I	R	E	D
A	N	O	N	■	L	I	N	E	N	■	A	R
B	E	N	■	F	A	V	O	R	■	U	S	E
E	R	■	T	A	K	E	N	■	B	L	E	W
L	I	G	H	T	E	R	■	M	I	L	■	■
■	■	H	I	N	■	■	R	E	T	A	I	N
S	T	O	N	E	■	L	A	D	E	■	R	E
T	E	S	■	S	H	I	N	E	■	M	O	S
P	A	T	■	S	E	E	K	S	■	A	N	T